TRUE BLOOD

AND

PHILOSOPHY

TRUE BLOOD

AND

PHILOSOPHY

WE WANNA THINK BAD THINGS
WITH YOU

Edited by
George A. Dunn and
Rebecca Housel

WILEY

John Wiley & Sons, Inc.

MERLOTTE'S MENU

ACKNOWLEDGMENTS

For the "Supes" We Just Can't Live Without

Rebecca Housel and George Dunn wish to thank the contributors of this book, as well as Bill Irwin, Connie Santisteban, Ellen Wright, and the entire Wiley team. Our hats also go off to Charlaine Harris, Alan Ball, and the many talented actors who brought *True Blood* to life.

George wishes to extend a giant thank-you to Bill Irwin, general editor of the series, for his tremendous support and encouragement. Special thanks also to Kevin Corn, who read an early draft of the introduction and whose comments were enormously helpful in making it better; Pamela Milam, who read and commented on some early drafts of chapters in this book; and his coeditor, Rebecca Housel, who taught him much about the process of editing. Most of all, he would like to thank Ariadne Blayde, for everything.

Rebecca wishes to dedicate her editorial work to the memory of her grandmothers, Eva (Masterman) Schwartz (Barson) and Mary Conley Thomas, women who meant as much to Rebecca as Sookie's Gran meant to her. She also wishes to thank Marguerite Schwartz, Bell Housel, Ethan Schwartz, Naomi Zack, Angela Belli, Monica Weis (SSJ), Michael Schwartz, and Bill Irwin for their many efforts on behalf of the book. Rebecca conveys gratitude to her beloved student-family for their love and support; she also wishes to recognize Gary Housel and Robert Housel for the same (and for putting up with incessant repeat viewings of *True Blood* episodes every week for the better part of a year). Rebecca's final appreciation goes out to Peter McLaren Black, MD, PhD; David Korones, MD; and Brett Shulman, MD, without whom she would simply not exist.

INTRODUCTION

"If a Tree Falls in the Woods, It's Still a Tree—Ain't It?"

When Amy Burley gives Jason Stackhouse a quick tutorial on the "circle of life" (you know, squirrels eating nuts, snakes eating squirrels, and so on), using the decor of Merlotte's as a visual aid, he exclaims, "Jesus Christ, I want to lick your mind!" Our boy Jason may be better known in Bon Temps for his good looks and "sex abilities," but it's phrases like "lick your mind" that draw fans to *True Blood*'s most earnest, if sometimes tragically misguided, seeker of life's meaning and purpose (or at least *his* life's meaning and purpose). In fact, "lick your mind" perfectly captures the blend of smarts and sensuality in the brilliant, sexually charged HBO series that inspired us to produce the book you hold in your hands, *True Blood and Philosophy*.

It all started with Charlaine Harris's *Dead until Dark*, published in 2001, which launched her series of critically acclaimed, best-selling supernatural mystery novels and introduced the world to a most unlikely sleuth, an attractive Louisiana barmaid and mind reader named Sookie Stackhouse. Harris's work caught the attention of Alan Ball, the award-winning screenwriter and director, who built his reputation on dark and daring works like *American Beauty* and *Six Feet Under*. With a healthy dose of edgy humor and deep compassion for his characters' frailties and foibles, Ball made a career of boldly delving into taboo subjects like death and transgressive sexuality, creating works that were brazen both in their unabashed carnality and in raising tough questions about the human condition. *True Blood*, Ball's adaptation of Harris's Southern Vampire Mystery novels, takes the same mind-licking approach as those earlier works. In the world of *True Blood*, as in the pages of Harris's novels, we encounter a wonderful array of richly drawn characters struggling to make sense of their bewildering world and their own sometimes equally bewildering desires and hungers. For those of us who hunger for insight and understanding, their stories offer a lavish banquet of philosophical morsels into which we can sink our proverbial fangs and from which we can draw both sustenance and delight.

As it turns out, philosophy has a lot in common with *True Blood*. Like the vampires, shapeshifters, and other supernatural beings that pass through Bon Temps, philosophers are often regarded as deviant characters due to their habit of overturning expectations and tempting us to think outside conventional boundaries. Like *True Blood*'s mind-reading detective Sookie Stackhouse, philosophers are unafraid to venture into dark corners of the human mind, where they sometimes unearth uncomfortable truths that others prefer to leave buried. And like the indomitable Jason Stackhouse, many philosophers engage in a quest for the meaning of life that often seems quixotic, an interminable pursuit that's been known to lead us down more than a few blind alleys—as Jason himself can testify. But like *True Blood* and Harris's novels, the philosophical quest can also be one of life's most delectable pleasures. Don't take our word for it, though. You hold the evidence in your hands.

When you surrender to the lure of *True Blood and Philosophy*, it won't cost you a drop of blood, but your perception of reality may be expanded and enriched so dramatically that you'll wonder whether you somehow ingested V-Juice. Okay, maybe that's too much to expect. But we *are* confident that your enjoyment of *True Blood* will be considerably enhanced by the time you spend with us pondering some of the more perplexing philosophical quandaries raised by the supernatural adventures of Sookie and her paranormal pals. For example, "pro-living" crusaders like the Reverend Steve Newlin denounce vampires as unnatural, but what does that really mean? If it's just another way of saying that vampires are evil, then why does evil exist in the first place? And can vampires—or any other creatures for that matter—be considered *inherently* evil?

Beyond these classic questions about the nature of evil, *True Blood* offers a fresh spin on the vampire genre that opens a rich vein of new philosophical queries. In the world envisioned by Ball and Harris, those conundrums-on-legs we call vampires have "come out of the coffin" and are attempting to live openly alongside human beings. Given the imbalance of power between human beings and vampires (who, in addition to superhuman strength and speed, also have a troubling knack for "glamouring" humans out of their free will), can humans and vampires belong to the same political community and participate in society as equals? Are the plights of gays and other minorities similar to the situation of *True Blood*'s vampires as they come out of the coffin and claim their place in the sun— um, better make that *in the shade*? The perennial evils of hatred, bigotry, and scapegoating—those not-so-supernatural scourges of our species—appear in a fresh light when their victims and perpetrators include not only ordinary human beings, but also vampires, shapeshifters, "fang-bangers," fanatical disciples of the Fellowship of the Sun, and, last but not least, a maenad as beguiling as she is depraved.

And let's not forget that the same show that stimulates our thinking with such succulent moral and metaphysical quandaries is also a wickedly sexy romp through the perilous precincts of love and lust. Could *True Blood* possibly have something to teach us about the paths and impediments to erotic fulfillment? Granted, most of us probably have desires considerably tamer than those of the more colorful denizens of Bon Temps, but still . . .

We don't promise that *True Blood and Philosophy* will supply the conclusive answers to all of these questions—or even to Jason's classic mindblower, "If a tree falls in the woods, it's still a tree—ain't it?" Philosophers have been debating questions like these since long before Godric was a twinkle in his maker's eye, and every answer has been shadowed by some doubt. It's the questioning itself that's mind-licking good. So invite us across your threshold. We want to *think* bad things with you!

PART ONE

"I USED TO HATE VAMPIRES, UNTIL I GOT TO KNOW ONE": VAMPIRE-HUMAN ETHICS

TO TURN OR NOT TO TURN

The Ethics of Making Vampires

Christopher Robichaud

Lorena: What more can I give? What is it you want
from me?
Bill: Choice.[1]

Sookie Stackhouse loves Bill Compton. And he loves her.
The trouble is, Bill is a vampire and Sookie is human. Well,
not quite, but she's not immortal either.[2] That means that as
Sookie ages, Bill won't. Let's suppose that despite her fairy
blood, Sookie can become a vampire. Would it be morally
permissible for Bill to turn her into one? This question lies
at the, um, heart of the issue we'll be looking at in this chapter.
The "unlife" of a vampire is often understood as something a
person is *condemned* to. Many see Bill, for instance, as being
damned to exist as a bloodthirsty creature of the night. Such
an existence sure doesn't sound like the kind of thing it would
be nice to bestow on another. This is one of the reasons we're

tempted to say that Bill acted wrongly when he forced Jessica Hamby to abandon her normal life and replace it with an unlife of drinking blood—or at least, of drinking TruBlood—and shunning the daylight.

Bill and Sookie, Sitting in a Coffin, K-i-s-s-i-n-g

There's an important difference between Jessica's being turned into a vampire and the possibility of Sookie's being turned into one. Jessica didn't give Bill her permission, her consent. In fact, she was quite vocal in communicating just how much she did not want to become a vampire. In contrast, it's likely that Sookie would be prepared to give her consent. (This may not be an entirely fair supposition, but it's not absurd, either. After all, at the end of the second season of *True Blood*, she does decide to accept Bill's marriage proposal.)[3] This particular difference between Jessica and Sookie seems morally relevant. Whether it's permissible for Bill to turn Sookie into a vampire—and, more generally, whether it's permissible for vampires to turn the living into the undead—seems to hinge on *consent*. By this way of thinking, a vampire can turn a living person into an undead one only if the person to be turned has given consent.

So there appears to be a fairly straightforward answer to the question of whether Bill is permitted to turn Sookie into a vampire. He's allowed to do so only if she gives him her consent. But like so much else in moral philosophy, this answer, even if correct, just scratches the surface of the issue.

Show Some Respect

Consent seems to be a necessary condition for the permissibility of Bill's turning Sookie into a vampire. But can we say more than this? Absolutely. The importance of consent in determining how we're allowed to treat others is a popular idea in moral philosophy and can be defended from several different perspectives. The one we'll focus on comes from one of the most famous philosophers of all time, Immanuel Kant (1724–1804). In his *Groundwork on the Metaphysics of Morals*, Kant presents a supreme moral principle, the categorical imperative, from which he thinks we can derive all of the more specific moral obligations that we have.[4] Kant provides several different formulations of this principle, perhaps the most popular one being the Formula of the End in Itself (also known as the Formula of Respect for Persons): "Act in such a way that you always treat humanity, whether in your own person or in the person of any other, never simply as a means, but always at the same time as an end."[5]

For Kant, we must treat persons this way—always as ends in themselves and never as mere means—because of their absolute, intrinsic value as agents who are capable of deliberating on their choices and setting their own goals. Our rational capacities are what make us distinct, claims Kant, and they ultimately ground the demands of morality. And so to respect the unconditional worth that all persons have as autonomous rational beings is to avoid using others to pursue *our* goals without their taking up those goals as their own. Let's suppose Bill wants to turn Sookie into a vampire so that they can spend eternity together. That's what Bill desires. And his desire leads him to adopt a goal: turn Sookie into a vampire. Now, it's likely that Bill is capable of doing this without so much as broaching the topic with Sookie, as we see him do with Jessica. But if he went about it in this way, he'd be doing something morally impermissible because it would violate the categorical imperative. Bill would be treating Sookie as a mere means to achieving his goal of turning her into a vampire. He'd be treating her as a mere means because he didn't allow her to take up his goal as her own—he didn't give her the respect she's owed as a rational person. To show Sookie proper respect, Bill would have to set aside his desire to turn her into a vampire until she *consented* to it.

According to this way of thinking, getting consent to perform certain actions is morally important because it's how we avoid treating people as mere means; it allows us, in other words, to have our actions conform to the categorical imperative. This isn't the only reason consent is important, but it's a compelling reason that stems from an appealing moral principle—the categorical imperative—and that acquires its force from an equally appealing idea—that people should be respected because of the unconditional worth they possess.

Read. My. Lips.

So Bill needs to get Sookie's consent before it's permissible for him to turn her into a vampire. But that's not the end of the story. One immediate question we need to answer is whether he needs to get her *explicit* consent. After all, there are plenty of cases where it seems that *tacit* or implicit consent is sufficient to guarantee that we aren't using people as a mere means and failing to give them the respect they're owed. Consider Sam Merlotte. As the owner and operator of Merlotte's Bar and Grill in Bon Temps, Sam is used all the time by customers to get what they want, typically food and drinks. They don't ask Sam's permission to do so, either. Yet it would be absurd to think that the Bon Temps community is doing something morally wrong by treating Sam in this way (although using Sam as a sacrifice to summon the "God Who Comes" is another story). It's reasonable for Sam's patrons to assume that he has tacitly consented to serving them food and drinks, since he freely established Merlotte's for just this purpose and, after all, he does take their money.

The point is that we use people all the time as a means to getting what we want, and there's usually nothing wrong with that. Problems arise only when we use them as *mere* means to our ends, when we use them without their consent. Often, tacit consent is sufficient to ensure that we're not going wrong in this way. In this light, should Bill presume that Sookie has tacitly consented to being turned into vampire if she agrees to marry him? The answer is no. Although there are many occasions where tacit consent is enough to ensure that we aren't treating people as a mere means, there are also plenty of times when explicit consent is needed. As a good rule of thumb, the more serious the action that's being considered, the less likely it is that tacit consent is enough.

Indeed, if we're looking for moral guidance, it seems like a very good idea to get explicit consent whenever there could be reasonable doubt about whether individuals are willing to take up our ends as their own. That's because even though there are many instances where tacit consent is given, there are also many cases where it assuredly is not. Certain men have claimed, for instance, that because a woman flirted with them while drinking, she tacitly consented to having sex with them, and so, when later in the evening she was found passed out on a bed, they were morally permitted to have sex with her. No way. Flirting with someone is absolutely *not* tacitly consenting to sex. And saying yes to a marriage proposal is not tacitly consenting to being turned into a vampire. We can make an even stronger statement: since the stakes are so high (pardon the pun) when it comes to becoming one of the undead, it seems plausible that tacit consent, even if present, is *never* sufficient to give a vampire permission to turn a living person into a creature of the night. If Bill wants to turn Sookie into a vampire, he needs to ask her directly and to hear "Yes" from her lips.

Look Before You Leap

But even this might not be enough. There's good reason to think that consent is going to do the moral work that we need it to do only if it is *informed* consent. Fangtasia is filled with vampire wannabes, folks whose heads are likely filled with one too many undead romance stories. Wanting to be creatures of the night, to Fangtasia they go. Happily, we know the sheriff of Area 5, Eric Northman, well enough to feel confident that he won't be granting any of them their wishes anytime soon. For Eric, it's doubtless because he loathes such people, and that's enough to keep him from even considering adding them to the vampire ranks. Whether he acknowledges it or not, however, Eric also has a good moral reason not to indulge their desires. That's because even though they've consented to being turned—quite often explicitly—they don't really know what they're consenting to. This robs the permission they give of its moral force. If their knowledge of vampires is based on flights of fancy rather than on the cold hard facts about existence as a bloodsucker, their uninformed verbal permission to be turned doesn't give Eric *moral* permission to turn them, whether he wants to or not.

Why? Recall the reason that consent is morally important. It's a way of making sure we're complying with the categorical imperative by helping us avoid treating persons as mere means to an end. Getting consent to do certain things to others is a way for us to give them the respect they deserve as rational agents. But we're not respecting their autonomy if their consent is given, as it were, "in the dark," regardless of whether we put them in the dark by deliberately deceiving them or they got there on their own. Accepting others' permission to do things to them while knowing full well that they don't have the relevant facts at hand is *not* respecting persons—it's manipulating them.

But even if we think this line of reasoning applies perfectly well to many of the patrons of Fangtasia, we might not think it applies to Bill and Sookie. After all, Sookie seems to have a grip on what the night-to-night ins and outs of being a vampire are all about. She's sleeping with one, for goodness' sake. More than that, she's been repeatedly drawn into the greater vampire community and exposed to how it operates. So it seems that if Sookie gives Bill her consent to be turned into a vampire, he needn't worry that it's uninformed.

Maybe. A problem with this way of seeing things arises when we acknowledge that there's some information we can't possess without experiencing it firsthand. For example, we can come to know lots of facts about free-falling by learning them from an instructor or a book, but we learn something new when we actually skydive. No matter how smart we are, we can't learn *what it's like* to free-fall out of a plane until we actually jump. Similarly, Sookie can't learn what it's like to be a vampire—to burn in daylight, to thirst for blood, to see the world through undead eyes—until she actually becomes one. So our worry is that Sookie's consent to be turned into a vampire won't have moral force unless it's informed, which would include knowing what it's like to be a vampire in this experiential sense. But she can't know that without already being a creature of the night! Hence, she can't give informed consent, and thus Bill doesn't have permission to turn her into a vampire.

The response to this line of reasoning is fairly obvious. It's too strong a condition to insist that the knowledge we possess be firsthand in order for our consent to morally count. If that were the case, wannabe skydivers would never end up sky-diving, because no instructor would ever be permitted to let them jump out of a plane, even after lots of pre-jump training— their informed consent could never be informed enough. That seems silly. Similarly, what counts as informed consent with regard to being turned into a vampire clearly falls somewhere between the wide-eyed romantic ignorance of the wannabes at Fangtasia and the unlife lessons learned from a century or more of existing as a vampire. Given Sookie's various connections to the vampire community, her consent to being turned may very well have enough knowledge behind it to be morally significant.

Don't Force It

We've seen that for consent to count morally it needs to be explicit and it needs to be informed. That's not all, however. It also can't be coerced. Consent given under duress doesn't carry any moral weight. Recall again that consent is important because it helps us make sure that we're giving persons the respect they are owed. Needless to say, we can't accomplish that by *forcing* people to give us permission to treat them in ways we want but they don't.

Some of the ways that consent can be coerced are not obvious. Consider the situation in which Lafayette Reynolds finds himself at the hands of Eric at the beginning of the second season of *True Blood*. Eric wasn't looking to turn Lafayette into a vampire, but if he had been, he didn't get permission to do so when Lafayette asked—begged, really—him for it. Lafayette by that point was under considerable emotional and physical duress. This is a straightforward example of an instance in which consent doesn't have moral force. But forced consent, or consent under duress, doesn't always look like the situation Lafayette was in. A situation of forced consent might not be traumatic at all; indeed, it might be anything but. One of the more interesting powers that vampires have is the ability to glamour persons—a powerful ability to *charm* them in a way that more or less forces the glamoured person to do anything the vampire wants. Sookie is immune to glamouring, so there's no worry that Bill would acquire her consent to be turned into a vampire by doing that to *her*. But Sookie is the exception. Would consent procured through glamouring carry moral weight? Clearly not, anymore than consent through hypnotism would. Part of why consent packs a moral punch is that it is given *freely*. We respect persons properly when we allow them to freely take up our ends as their own. But surely a necessary condition for genuine consent is that the person giving consent is not under the mental control of another. So vampires can't circumvent the moral demands of genuine consent by glamouring someone into providing it.

Exceptions to the Rule?

Maybe we're being too restrictive. Are there perhaps situations in which a vampire would be morally permitted to forgo getting explicit, informed, noncoercive consent before turning a living person into a vampire? From our reasoning so far, it sure seems like the answer is no. But that may burden us with some results that are hard to live with. One involves Jessica. Jessica vehemently resisted Bill's turning her into a vampire. But it's not entirely crazy to think that Jessica is better off existing as an undead creature of the night than she would have been had she continued living the life she was born into. After all, vampirism has empowered Jessica in a way that her family was never able to. Let's suppose, for the sake of argument, that Jessica is in fact better off now than she would have been and also that only by becoming a vampire could she be better off. If we're serious about the moral importance of consent, we're committed to saying that Bill shouldn't have made Jessica better off. And that sure seems troubling on the surface of things. But only on the surface.

Although we have a moral obligation to make people better off, we don't have a moral obligation to make them better off *no matter what*. The *no matter what* in this case involves treating Jessica as a mere means. Ultimately, where we come down on this depends on how strongly we take the moral mandate to give people the respect owed to them. If we think this mandate isn't nearly as absolute as Kant thought it was, then perhaps it will matter to us that Jessica would have been worse off had Bill not chosen to use her as a mere means to his own ends. But if we share Kant's conviction that we have an overriding duty to respect the autonomy of others, then we'll be more comfortable accepting that sometimes making someone better off, while certainly a good thing, is nevertheless not what morally ought to be done. In the case of Jessica, we might present our reasoning this way. Granted that she's better off as a vampire than as a human being, she nevertheless expressed her desire to remain mortal. Bill should have respected her right, as a rational agent, to make her own decisions, even if they may be bad ones. And, besides, no attempt was made to present her with facts that might have persuaded her to embrace an unlife. No one gave her an opportunity to deliberate, nor did anyone take her lack of consent seriously. For these reasons (and more), what Bill did was wrong, regardless of whether Jessica gained a better existence than what she had before.

It would be convenient to leave things right there and conclude by saying that Jessica's case shows that consent is always needed. But we wouldn't be doing serious moral philosophy if we didn't go a little further and end by muddying the waters a bit. One thing that makes the reasoning just presented persuasive is that Jessica was never given a chance to deliberate adequately on becoming a vampire. But what if there's no such chance to give? What if a vampire faces the choice of turning someone or letting him die right then and there? The obvious example that comes to mind is Eric and his sire, Godric.[6] Godric had his eye on Eric for quite some time but turned him only after Eric had suffered a fatal wound on the battlefield. For a variety of reasons, it's reasonable to assume that Eric was in no condition to give adequate consent to being turned into a vampire. It's also reasonable to assume that Eric is better off continuing to exist as a vampire than he would have been dying on the battlefield. Did Godric still do something wrong?

Here we may have room to suggest that he didn't. The general thought process is as follows: If explicit consent at a certain time *can't* be given, but it is reasonable to conclude that it *would* have been given had there been the opportunity, then, everything else being equal, you haven't failed to treat a person with the appropriate moral respect by acting *as if* consent were given. We use this principle when, for example, we allow loved ones to make certain medical decisions for a patient who's unable to make decisions for himself. For this principle to apply to Godric, he must *reasonably* believe that Eric would have given the appropriate sort of consent had he been able to do so. Did Godric have good grounds to believe this? We can't really know. But it's not too hard to give him the benefit of the doubt. He is, after all, an ancient vampire who's genuinely sympathetic to the human condition.

Except in such rare circumstances, though, vampires need explicit, informed, noncoercive consent before they're permitted to turn the living into the undead. Bill must get this kind of permission from Sookie before having her join him in a state of undeath. And he ought to atone somehow for making Jessica into a creature of the night without her consent. Bill has a lot to do and a lot to think about. But then he always does. He has set himself upon the path of being a morally upright vampire—not the easiest course, to say the least.

NOTES

1. Episode 207, "Release Me."

2. The first two seasons of *True Blood* hint that Sookie isn't human. We learn from Charlaine Harris's Southern Vampire Mysteries that Sookie has fairy blood in her veins.

3. In Harris's novels, Sookie's relationship with Bill doesn't develop quite so nicely, especially after Bill reveals to her that he initially wooed her on orders from the queen of Louisiana.

4. Immanuel Kant., *The Moral Law: Groundwork on the Metaphysics of Morals*, trans. Hiram Paton (New York: Routledge, 2005).

5. Ibid., p. 66.

6. Godric is Eric's sire only in the *True Blood* television series, not in Charlaine Harris's novels, from which the series was adapted.

DRESSING UP AND PLAYING HUMAN

Vampire Assimilation in the Human Playground

Jennifer Culver

"Sookie, you have to understand that for hundreds, thousands of years we [vampires] have considered ourselves better than humans, separate from humans." He thought for a second. "Very much in the same relationship to humans as humans have to, say, cows. Edible like cows, but cute, too."

I was knocked speechless. I had sensed this, of course, but to have it spelled out was just . . . nauseating. Food that walked and talked, that was us. McPeople.

—Eric to Sookie[1]

Leave it to Eric Northman to tell it like it is. Smart humans in the world of the Southern Vampire Mysteries and *True Blood*, its HBO incarnation, never forget for a moment that when vampires are "mainstreaming," they are at play, playing at being human. To create a more even playground, vampires perpetuate certain myths, such as their supposed adverse reactions to crucifixes and their inability to be photographed, in order to appear weaker than they really are. Through play, vampires who desire to mainstream learn the ins and outs of human society. Meanwhile, humans gain a less threatening, less fearful impression of vampires. In the realm of play, vampires who don't follow the rules of mainstreaming (we'll call them spoilsports) threaten the fragile boundaries of a society where human beings and vampires (and shifters, too) interact.

When vampires announced their existence to the world, crossing the boundary from myth to reality, their strategy was to appeal to human beings as much as possible by appearing to be nonthreatening. Spokespersons were chosen for their attractiveness, their humanlike mannerisms, and their general appeal. The "virus" explanation for the unique attributes of vampires encourages human beings to be less afraid of their undead neighbors. Because vampires want to live with human beings rather than looming menacingly over them, success depends on their ability to play human.

Play to Learn, Play to Live

> It was so normal! I beamed with pride. When Bill first started coming into Merlotte's, the atmosphere had been on the strained side. Now, people came and went casually, speaking to Bill or only nodding, but not making a big issue of it either way.
>
> —Sookie[2]

Bill Compton's acceptance depends on an act of play: he must pretend to be human to be accepted by human beings. Beneath the surface, both vampires and human beings know the truth. Vampires are incredibly strong and ferocious, and they have the power to glamour. Humans, by contrast, have strong emotions, vitality, and the much-desired blood. Even with the availability of synthetic blood, human blood continues to tempt the vampires, especially when they're very hungry or in a heightened state of arousal. For mainstreaming to work, both sides must be willing to put aside disturbing differences and treat one another as equals.

To see how this can work, let's consider a definition of play offered by the philosopher John Huizinga (1872–1945). Play, he said, "is a voluntary activity or occupation occurring within certain fixed limits of time and place, according to rules freely accepted but absolutely binding, having its aim in itself and accompanied by a feeling of tension, joy, and the consciousness that it is 'different' from 'ordinary life.'"[3] Successful mainstreaming for vampires depends on how well they can play the game of being human. This is why Bill orders red wine his first night in Merlotte's when he learns that Sam Merlotte hadn't yet stocked synthetic blood. He understands that a person should be seen drinking when in a bar.

Vampires don't just play when they're mainstreaming. Vampire culture actually revolves around "courtesy and custom," according to Bill, even when vampires are the only ones present. Because they "have to live together for centuries," the rules and traditions vampires create help maintain a sense of structure, keeping the vampire world secure and familiar even as the outside world continues to change. These courtesies and customs represent the "crystallized" and residual elements of the acts of play that helped shape the culture in the first place.[4] For their rules and traditions to carry any weight, vampires must agree to perpetuate them. As Sookie Stackhouse enters the vampire world more deeply, she finds herself learning about sheriffs, queens, and kings. In *Club Dead*, the third book of the Southern Vampire Mysteries, Sookie's heart breaks as she learns that the rules of that world dictate that Bill must leave her to answer the call of his maker.

Do all vampires play by the rules? Of course not. Some vampires cheat, just like some human beings. Others act as "spoilsports," a term Huizinga uses for a figure who "shatters the play-world itself" by revealing the "relativity and fragility of the play-world in which he had temporarily shut himself with others."[5] Some call this "going rogue." Mickey in *Dead as a Doornail*, the fifth book of the Southern Vampire Mysteries, is a prime example of a rogue vampire. Vampires discourage going rogue by punishing the spoilsport or leaving him unprotected from other vampires and creatures of the night. Safety lies in the hierarchy and courtesies of vampire culture, in playing the game.

Engaging in play has certain requirements: boundaries that mark off the arena of play in space and time, rules to create a sense of order, and specific goals to accomplish. Participation in play forges a bond between players. As all leave the playing field, they carry away a private shared experience, for no one outside the play will truly understand the inner workings of the game. Consequently, whether a vampire wants to mainstream or make an appearance at Fangtasia, he had better know the rules of each play-world. And the first rule is to know the boundaries.

Thresholds and Invitations

> I was going to have to rescind his invitation to enter. What had stopped me from that drastic step before— what stopped me now—was the idea that if I ever needed help, and he couldn't enter, I might be dead before I could yell, "Come in!"
>
> —Sookie[6]

Just because a vampire wants to mainstream, that doesn't mean that he acts human all the time. To the contrary, the mainstreaming vampire knows the appropriate behavior for each human encounter. This just makes sense since not all humans expect the same things from a vampire interaction. The fang-bangers at the bars want to be a little scared and a little wowed by the vampire experience, which is why Eric requires vampires in his area to appear at the bar in shifts. Other humans, like patrons at Merlotte's, prefer their vampires to behave as humanly as possible. In either case, the vampire must adjust his behavior accordingly when crossing the boundary into human territory.

In play theory, the boundary sets the limits for play in time and place. Like a ritual, which Huizinga regards as a sacred act of play, the boundary creates hallowed space and is a "temporary world" dedicated to the performative act. Huizinga lists several types of boundaries, including a stage, a tennis court, and a court of law.[7] Crossing the boundary line indicates a willingness to participate in play for a specified time in that space. Even a gameboard can reflect a boundary, as the rules apply only to the time and place of the game played on it.

In Sookie's world the actual threshold of a human being's home serves as one of the most powerful boundary markers between the human and vampire worlds. Vampires can enter public places at will, but only an invitation from the owner can admit a vampire into the home. Sookie learns this early on and uses this knowledge to her advantage throughout the series. When weary of vampire politics and posturing in *Club Dead*, she rescinds Bill's and Eric's invitations into her home, forcing them to walk backward out the door against their will. Realizing that she was finally at peace and that the deadly vampires were trapped outside her door, Sookie reports that she "hadn't laughed so hard in weeks." In *Dead as a Doornail* Sookie rescinds the invitation of the rogue vampire Mickey. This time, however, it's not for amusement but to save her life. With Eric hurt and unable to help, Sookie realizes the only way to save herself and her friend Tara Thornton is to force Mickey to leave.

In the vampire world, kings, queens, and sheriffs rule over certain territories with clear boundaries. Vampire officials can be quite territorial and expect to be informed of all vampire activity in the area. That's why in *Living Dead in Dallas* and *Club Dead*, the second and third books of the Southern Vampire Mysteries, Eric dons a disguise to keep an eye on Sookie in Dallas and Jackson when he sends her on missions to those cities (she is his property, after all). Had he entered Dallas or Jackson uninvited as Eric Northman, the sheriffs and others in those regions might have taken the action as an insult or, even worse, as an act of aggression. In the language of Huizinga's play theory, Eric's impersonation constitutes cheating, an attempt to skirt the rules, which is nonetheless different from being a spoilsport like Mickey. At least the cheater acknowledges that rules and boundaries are in place. He treats the boundaries as real and significant, even as he crosses over them. Wearing his disguise, Eric pretends to be playing the game and honoring the boundary markers. At no time do the vampires in Dallas or Jackson realize that their boundaries were breached by the sheriff of Area 5.

Rules: What It Means to Be "Mine"

> "I seem to be having sex with you in a closet," Bill said in a subdued voice. "Did you, ah, volunteer?"
>
> —Bill[8]

Within the boundaries lie specific rules for play. Breaking a rule means the collapse of play until order is restored. When the twentieth-century philosopher Roger Callois expanded on Huizinga's theory of play, he explained that even playing *make-believe* implies rules, the main rule being that all will agree to act *as if* this make-believe world were real.[9] The main rule that must be followed for vampire mainstreaming to be successful is the same rule that governs all make-believe play: vampires must act *as if* they are human. What's so hard about that? Vampires were once human, right? Let's consider this notion of being human.

"Human" in this case is more than a biological designation. To be human in our sense of the term requires participation in a way of life shaped by the rules of human society. Vampires are expected to mimic the customs, manners, emotions, and behaviors of the human beings around them. As human culture changes over time, vampires must adjust. In *Dead until Dark*, the first book of the Southern Vampire Mysteries, Bill learns from Arlene's children that a true boyfriend would bring Sookie flowers. Throughout their courtship, Sookie attempts to reconcile Bill's actions, including his protectiveness and his habit of treating her like a "kept woman," with how she believes a boyfriend *should* act. More than once in the novels, Sookie notes that Bill has never proposed, as if even this gesture, empty as it would be since vampires and humans cannot marry (this is true in the novels, but not in the HBO series), reflects her conception of what a romantic relationship should be like. Elsewhere in the novels, Eric expresses his belief that Jason Stackhouse should be more protective of his sister, Sookie, citing older ideas about gender roles and family duty. Keeping up with the times must be hard for vampires.

Age equals power for vampires, but age also presents problems for vampires who want to play human. Bill reports that the longer he remains a vampire, the harder it is for him to remember what it was like to be human. Vampires like Eric, who are even older than Bill, seem to lack what most of us would consider humanity in any form. In *Dead as a Doornail*, for example, Sookie has to explain to Eric why he should care about Tara's enslavement to Mickey. Many of the healings Sookie receives from the vampires occur purely as reciprocation for services she has rendered or risks she has taken on their behalf, not because the vampires (with the exception of Bill) feel any real sense of caring for her.

For a vampire to refuse to act human in a human setting is the act of a spoilsport. The spoilsport ruins play because he shatters the illusion, not just by breaking the rules but by reminding everyone that the experience isn't real but is just play. In an early episode of *True Blood*, the roguish vampire Malcolm calls Bill "everyone's favorite buzz kill," on account of his mainstreaming goals, and Diane reminds him that "not everyone wants to dress up and play human."[10] Malcolm and Diane live in a vampire nest, a group of vampires who may live together for centuries and become unusually close. Nested vampires often call one another "brother" or "sister" and reject mainstreaming. When Malcolm, Diane, and Liam (the other vampire in their nest) show up at Merlotte's, they menace and offend the patrons of the bar, pretty much just by acting like vampires and treating the human beings in the bar as part of a lower order of creature. Their actions make it harder for the patrons to accept Bill, despite his effort to keep the peace, because their actions confirm their worst stereotypes and fears about vampires.

Spoilsports exist on the human side as well. The Fellowship of the Sun is an organization of spoilsports, human beings who don't believe that vampire mainstreaming, not to mention the very existence of vampires, is a good idea. Their opposition is so zealous that they are willing to kill Sookie because of her association with vampires. Many of Merlotte's patrons also look down on Sookie for dating a vampire, believing that a good girl wouldn't act that way. (But, with the exception of the mentally unhinged Rene Lenier, none of them are necessarily ready to kill her for that indiscretion.) On a larger scale, spoilsports are responsible for laws that forbid vampires and humans to marry each other (except in Vermont, according to the show), although vampires have achieved some rights since they "came out of the coffin."

Vampires live under a strict code of rules in their own world as well, as Sookie glimpses when, for her own safety, Bill announces to the other vampires that "she's mine." This designation shields Sookie from the designs of other vampires, regardless of whether she lets Bill actually drink from her. In return for her safety, she must endure being regarded as a possession, even to the point of being called Bill's pet by some of his vampire associates.

Sookie's association with the vampires forces her to abide by more and more of their rules. Like Bill, she must answer a summons from Eric whenever he has a need for her, which has taken her away from her home and placed her in peril many times. In *Club Dead*, she allows Russell Edgington to lick blood from her wound, knowing that act to be a courtesy she should extend to this vampire king regardless of how distasteful she finds it. Why can't Sookie be a spoilsport and refuse? Because unlike the vampires who make trouble at Merlotte's, she doesn't have enough power. The vampires could destroy the bar if they feel so inclined. The bar patrons know it and so feel forced to tolerate the vampires' bad behavior in exchange for their safety. But Sookie can't destroy anyone at Club Dead. As useful as her telepathic gifts may be at times, they do not grant her the physical power she would need to fight her way out of a bad encounter with a vampire.

The Goals of Play

"We are not human. We can pretend to be, when we're trying to live with people . . . in your society. We can sometimes remember what it was like to be among you, one of you. But we are not the same race. We are no longer of the same clay."

—Bill[11]

Play occurs for a reason. Huizinga believes that participants enter into play to be able to achieve something. Callois later categorizes types of play by the types of goals attached to the specific activity, differentiating games of competition (such as chess or soccer) from games of chance (such as roulette or flipping a coin) or games of simulation or mimicry (such as theater).[12] If play, as Huizinga argues, shapes the greater culture, then we, as cultural players, enter into each interaction, from the classroom to the grocery store, with a goal in mind. In public play-worlds, such as bars, shopping centers, and schools, people sometimes enter with unique goals that may conflict with those of others. Conflicting goals can lead to tensions within the play-world that can be resolved within the game, provided all players follow the rules of the space (such as the bar). In a public space such as Merlotte's Bar and Grill, people come in for a variety of reasons. Sookie comes to work and rarely socializes at the bar, so her goal is to earn money. To achieve her goal, Sookie often pastes on a fake smile, tries to tune out the unwelcome and often offensive thoughts of patrons, and quickly hustles food and drink to her stations in hope of better tips. Except on the rare occasion when she has some additional goal, like listening for incriminating thoughts in order to clear her brother, Jason, from suspicion of murder, as in *Dead until Dark*, almost all of her actions at Merlotte's can be explained in terms of her moneymaking goal.

Patrons in the bar arrive with different goals, but they're rarely in conflict. Most go to drink and socialize. Jason and Hoyt Fortenberry come in to blow off steam after a hard day at work. Andy Bellefleur takes Halleigh Robinson out for a meal. Bill can't drink wine, but he orders some anyway on his first foray into the bar because, as we observed earlier, he understands that this is the thing to do when you're in a bar, especially if you show up alone with no one to engage immediately in conversation. Bill's goal is to mainstream and not necessarily to drink, so when he orders wine from Sookie, it's in an attempt to fit in. Once Merlotte's begins stocking synthetic blood, Bill can mainstream and drink at the same time, and he often does.

Bill's desire to mainstream leads to other unexpected decisions. In *Living Dead in Dallas*, he appears out and about with Portia Bellefleur to assist her murder investigation but also to further his mainstreaming process. He knows that Portia does not care much for him and has her own agenda and goals, but he goes to football games and other places with her, understanding that it's good to appear in public in the company of a human. Likewise, he speaks to a meeting of the Descendants of the Glorious Dead in order to mainstream and to please Sookie and her grandmother. Bill's goal of a mainstreamed life hits obstacles only when his vampire obligations interfere.

Eric's mainstreaming goals carry more limited expectations, as he wants to mainstream only when it profits him. Eric's actions make sense in light of his true goal of maintaining power. In *Club Dead*, he seems to act like a better boyfriend than Bill when he sends a crew to replace Sookie's gravel driveway after she complains about it, but he does so with his own ulterior motives in mind, and Sookie knows it. In fact, Sookie comes closest to trusting Eric only after Eric has been cursed with amnesia in *Dead to the World*, the fourth of the Southern Vampire Mysteries, because he no longer remembers how he used to act and begins showing raw human emotions, such as fear and love.

Sookie realizes that others around her have goals that are independent of hers. That's why she's not judgmental of Jason's playboy ways, Sam's shapeshifting, or Arlene's desire to find the next perfect husband. She is irritated most often when people don't make their motives clear from the beginning. Had the werewolf Alcide Herveaux told her that he needed her to use her telepathic abilities at the funeral of Colonel Flood in *Dead as a Doornail*, she likely still would have attended the event as a favor to him. But because Alcide hid his true intentions and couched his request as a desire for her company, she responded with anger and disappointment. Unfortunately, honesty like Sookie's is a rare thing in her world, maybe even in any world.

Play Changes the Player

"But, in a way you're like lions."

Eric looked astonished. "Lions?" he said weakly.

"Lions all kill stuff." At the moment, this idea seemed like an inspiration. "So you're predators, like lions and raptors. But you use what you kill. You have to kill to eat."

"The catch in that comforting theory being that we look almost exactly like you. And we used to be you. And we can love you, as well as feed off you. You could hardly say the lion wanted to caress the antelope."

—Sookie to Eric[13]

Play creates significance out of a lack of seriousness. While Huizinga believes that the social order and its institutions all stem from play, we also return to playful activities to feel revitalized and significant again. No other activity fulfills this need in such a profound way. A social activity, play draws individuals out of seclusion and encourages them to participate in the world through a variety of roles. The public "coming out" of vampires provides both them and human beings with the opportunity to play new kinds of games. Vampires can mainstream in the human world, acting mostly human in human settings. And by watching vampires, human beings gain an understanding and partial access to a world previously unknown to them.

All players leave the game forever changed by the experience, having forged a bond with others on the playing field. That bond is why Sookie can't ignore Eric's running down the road in the middle of night in *Dead to the World* and why Bill still wants to protect Sookie even after their romantic relationship ends. Bit by bit, exposure to mainstreaming vampires like Bill Compton and the spokespersons for the American Vampire League, like Nan Flanagan, convince human beings that the presence of vampires isn't all bad. As long as human beings stay in their human setting, this new positive image of the vampire can become predominant. But once human beings enter the boundaries of the vampire world, the rules of the human playground disappear and things get dangerous.

NOTES

1. Charlaine Harris, *Dead as a Doornail* (New York: Ace Books, 2005), p. 214.
2. Charlaine Harris, *Living Dead in Dallas* (New York: Ace Books, 2002), p. 62.
3. Johan Huizinga, *Homo Ludens* (New York: Routledge, 2008), p. 28.
4. Ibid., p. 46.
5. Ibid., p. 11.
6. Charlaine Harris, *Club Dead* (New York: Ace Books, 2003), p. 34.
7. Huizinga, *Homo Ludens*, p. 10.
8. Harris, *Club Dead*, p. 224.
9. Roger Callois, *Man, Play and Games* (Chicago: Univ. of Illinois Press, 2001).
10. Episode 103, "Mine."
11. Harris, *Living Dead in Dallas*, p. 232.
12. Callois, *Man, Play and Games*, p. 36. Callois also includes games of "vertigo," from children whirling around to the more structured waltz.
13. Charlaine Harris, *Dead to the World* (New York: Ace Books, 2005), p. 53.

PETS, CATTLE, AND HIGHER LIFE FORMS ON *TRUE BLOOD*

Ariadne Blayde and George A. Dunn

"You know they can hypnotize you," Tara Thornton warns Sookie Stackhouse, alerting her to one of the dangers of associating with vampires. "Yeah," Sookie responds sarcastically, "and black people are lazy and Jews have horns."[1] Sookie rejects intolerance with a wave of her hand, comparing prejudice against vampires with other detestable forms of discrimination, such as racism and anti-Semitism. But as we know, not all of the residents of Bon Temps have such an open-minded attitude. It's no coincidence that the show is set in the Deep South, where only a few short decades ago the civil rights movement put an end to racial segregation and the disenfranchisement of African American voters, or that the first actual vampire we see on the show is Nan Flanagan, spokesperson for the American Vampire League (AVL), clamoring for equal rights. And, of course, the sign reading "God hates fangs," which we see in the opening credit sequence, echoes the slogan of the blinkered bigot Fred Phelps, "God hates fags."

Clearly, when vampires came out of the coffin, they brought with them the seeds of a whole new era of prejudice. Yet the prejudice against vampires is reminiscent of many other forms of intolerance and discrimination with which we're all too familiar. On the AVL Web site, we even find a letter from Nan addressed to supporters of vampire equality, in which she signs off by explicitly evoking the memory of the civil rights movement with a quote from the Reverend Martin Luther King Jr.: "The arc of the universe is long. But it bends toward justice."[2]

And Justice for All—Human Beings?

Throughout most of the long arc of human history, however, justice has been considered something we owe only to other *human* beings. No doubt that's one of the reasons the AVL has ads stressing how "vampires were people too," featuring attractive vampires who are in every respect indistinguishable from ordinary human beings. These ads seem to be based on the gambit that if the rest of us can be persuaded that vampires are really just an exotic variety of human being—or at least close enough to be granted honorary human status—then we'll be more inclined to extend to them *human* rights. Although a vampire like Bill Compton's neighbor Diane would surely sneer at this approach as a case of vampires wanting "to dress up and play human," it's not hard to understand why the AVL would adopt this strategy of representing vampires as human, more or less.[3] After all, vampires have been around for a long time, certainly long enough to have noticed that throughout history one of the chief justifications offered for depriving some groups, like women or racial minorities, of their rights is that they are supposedly somehow *less* than fully human.

We wish we could say that philosophers played no part in this shameful history of denying justice to certain groups deemed subhuman, but that's not the case. Aristotle (384–322 B.C.E.), for instance, was one of the greatest philosophers of the ancient world—of all time, really—a genius whose thinking has shaped Western civilization in ways too numerous to count. He was also the author of the classical definition of human beings as "the rational animals," our possession of rational intellects supposedly elevating us above every other species.[4] It was our superior rationality that Aristotle believed gave us the right to exploit all the other animals, who "exist for the sake of man, the tame for use and food, the wild, if not all, at least the greater part of them, for food, and for the provision of various instruments."[5] Immediately after making this claim, though, Aristotle added that just as we may hunt nonhuman animals, we are equally entitled to "hunt" and enslave other human beings, such as the "barbarians" whom the Greeks regarded as their inferiors. The allegedly defective reasoning abilities of these non-Greek peoples reduced them to the same status as beasts and made them fair game for exploitation. And sadly, Aristotle offered a similar justification for the oppression of women, whom he judged to be wanting in reason, deficient in humanity, and thus naturally subordinate to men.

Notice that in both cases—slaves and women—the argument for denying their rights depended on denying their full humanity and lumping them in with other nonhuman creatures who, in the mind of Aristotle and his successors, existed only to be exploited by full-fledged human beings. Ever since, privileged groups have sought to justify the oppression of women and minorities by claiming that they are somehow less than human. When a Republican activist recently thought it was clever to quip that a gorilla who had escaped from the zoo was an ancestor of our African American first lady, he was only the latest in a long line of racists defending their privileges by insinuating that members of minority groups aren't quite as human as them.

Aristotle believed that reason set us apart from our fellow creatures, crowning us as their rightful rulers and reducing them to the status of servants and instruments, whom we could use as means for whatever ends we choose. Other philosophers agreed that human beings occupied a unique niche in the order of things that gave us unlimited rights over other creatures, even if some of these philosophers have defined our distinctiveness in terms different from Aristotle's. Christian philosophers, for example, were drawn to the idea that human beings were created in "the likeness of God." Because we bear a divine image, we are connected in a special way to God and related to a supernatural or divine reality that transcends the merely natural world. We may be animals, but we're also somehow *more* than animals through our connection to the divine. In the opinion of many Christian philosophers such as Thomas Aquinas (1225–1274), this divine connection invests us with sovereign authority over the rest of the creation. "It matters not how man behaves to animals," he argued, "because God has subjected all things to man's power."[6] Steve Newlin would undoubtedly cheer this sentiment and insist that it applies even more to our relationship with "soulless" creatures like vampires.

Immanuel Kant (1724–1804), one of the greatest philosophers of the modern era, also believed that we had the right to exploit nonhuman animals. And, like many of the religious philosophers who came before him, he believed that we enjoyed that right because we somehow transcended the limits of the natural world to which other creatures were subject. For Kant, however, our transcendence consisted of our *moral autonomy*, our not being subject to the tyranny of those instincts and inclinations to which he believed every other creature remained enslaved. We were unique, he believed, in being able to follow the dictates of morality instead. Referring to the value of moral autonomy, he wrote that "morality, and humanity insofar as it is capable of morality, is that which alone has dignity."[7] As creatures possessing dignity, we're entitled to be treated with respect, as ends in ourselves whose happiness and well-being ought to matter to others. Anything else, however, is a mere *thing* that exists only to be used by human beings as a means to an end. Lacking dignity, these things—including nonhuman animals—possess a different kind of value that's conditional on the uses we make of them, a value that Kant calls their *price*.

How Much Is a Vampire Worth?

For centuries popular culture and folklore have featured vampires feeding on human beings, but *True Blood* introduces the idea that human beings can exploit vampires as well. Vampire blood, or V, is what Lafayette Reynolds calls "pure, undiluted, 24-karat *life*"—which is more than a little ironic given that it comes from the bodies of creatures who are ostensibly dead.[8] But regardless of its source, V has immense power as an aphrodisiac for human beings, stimulating the senses and connecting the user with a deeper, richer, more beautiful reality. Like the fur trade, which destroys animals with no regard for any worth they may have as conscious beings, dealing in V has ethical implications that are questionable to say the least. Because their bodies possess this desirable substance, vampires become a valuable commodity for human beings. When Denise Rattray meets Bill, Sookie telepathically hears her mentally calculate Bill's monetary *price* based on how much blood she and her husband can drain from him: "Holy shit, almost two hundred ounces . . . that's ten thousand dollars, sweet Jesus!" Horrified by what the Rattrays plan to do to this innocent vampire, Sookie is determined to save him. "It's not like siphoning gas out of a car!" she explains to her brother, Jason.[9]

Amy Burley thinks otherwise. With Jason's reluctant assistance, she kidnaps the reclusive, soft-spoken vampire Eddie Gauthier so that she can have a supply of V handy at all times. Eddie is burned with silver, denied nourishment, and chained to a metal chair with silver that prevents him from moving and causes him tremendous pain. For all intents and purposes, this is torture, but it's not much different from the way millions of animals are treated every day on factory farms, where, like

Eddie, they are viewed as mere things whose sole value lies in the monetary value that can be extracted from the tortures they undergo. On factory farms, animals are often confined for most of their lives in crates so small they can't even turn around. Many of them never see daylight or inhale fresh air; and they are injected with a plethora of chemicals in order to prime them for human consumption.[10] Eddie, like the animals on factory farms, is exploited as a commodity with no regard for his suffering.

How can Amy justify treating Eddie this way? He's more or less a regular guy—he has hopes and regrets, he feels fear and pain, and he likes to watch *Heroes*. Recognizing these simple and obvious facts, Jason refuses to continue using him as a means to an end. But to Amy, none of that matters. In her mind, there is one sacrosanct prerequisite to being treated like a valuable individual—being human. No matter how much evidence there may be that Eddie suffers just as greatly as any human being would in the same circumstances, no matter how incontrovertible it is that he regards his existence as no less an end in itself than does any human being, Amy is incapable of seeing him as anything other than a thing to be exploited, a disposable commodity. Why? For no reason other than that he's a vampire and not a human being.

Although Eddie is clearly a sentient, feeling being, Amy is entirely comfortable torturing him simply because he is not one of her kind. This is a classic example of speciesism, the belief that only members of our own species are entitled to respect or moral consideration. And although there are no vampires to exploit in our society, attitudes and practices similar to Amy's are common with respect to nonhuman animals.

Vampires as Higher Life Forms

Philosophers such as Aristotle, Aquinas, and Kant all imagined a rigid partition running through the natural world. On one side stood human beings, the lone possessors of reason, divine grace, moral autonomy, or some other rare and precious attribute that entitled us to moral consideration. On the other side of the fence were crowded all of the other creatures, an extraordinarily diverse menagerie that included chimpanzees, gorillas, dolphins, donkeys, dogs, elephants, lizards, snakes, catfish, sharks, lobsters, spiders, termites, dragonflies, and sea anemones. Somehow this heterogeneous assortment of creatures was thought to comprise a distinct class separated by a taxonomic abyss from humanity, as though highly intelligent and gregarious chimpanzees and gorillas shared more in common with sea anemones than either shared with human beings, their close biological cousins. Even as evidence accumulates that some of these creatures possess many of the same traits that have traditionally been thought to be the sole preserve of our own species, such as the capacity for language and reason or a sense of fairness, the belief that moral consideration is owed to human beings alone persists.[11]

Given these attitudes, it's no surprise that the AVL would want to persuade the world that vampires really are (or *were*) as human the next guy. The irony is that many—maybe even most—vampires actually regard human beings as lower forms of life ripe for exploitation, not much different from the way Aristotle and others regarded nonhuman species. Vampires may face intolerance and contempt from human beings, but the bad blood runs both ways, as both groups bandy about derogatory terms for each other—vampires may be "fangers," but human beings are "breathers" and "bloodbags." Many human beings may see vampires as soulless and morally depraved, but there's also a strong sentiment among vampires that they are in fact the superior ones. Moreover, they appear to have considerable justification for this view of themselves. For starters, vampires are much stronger and faster than human beings. Bill, for example, destroys the Rattrays' trailer with the force of a tornado, and he's always doing that creepy thing where one second he's across the room and the next thing you know he's right in your face. But impressive as these abilities are, they wouldn't be enough to upset the conviction of philosophers like Aristotle, Aquinas, or Kant that human beings are the crown of creation. These philosophers never based that claim on humanity's physical prowess anyway. After all, much of the animal kingdom clearly has us beat in that department. By and large, philosophers have thought that humanity's superiority lies elsewhere, in our supposedly unmatched cognitive talents, which afford us a richer experience of the world and maybe even, as many religious thinkers claim, a pipeline to some sort of transcendent reality.

On this view, the more sophisticated the mental equipment the greater the value of the life. For a measure of how prevalent this belief is, consider that even Peter Singer, the philosopher and animal rights advocate who first popularized the term *speciesism*, has argued that human lives are worth more than those of other animals, because our richer capacity for experience means that something of greater value is lost when one of us perishes. "It is not arbitrary," he writes, "to hold that the life of a self-aware being, capable of abstract thought, of planning for the future, of complex acts of communication, and so on, is more valuable than the life of a being without those capacities."[12] Human superiority, in this view, lies not in our physical abilities but in the quality of our minds.

But here as well vampires leave us in the dirt. They're not only endowed with extremely heightened senses, but their experience of the world is intense and complex in ways that far surpass anything ordinarily available to our dull and meager human faculties. Sookie discovers this for herself after she drinks Bill's blood and gains some access to the world as he experiences it. Even a bite of sausage at breakfast becomes a revelatory adventure in which the underlying connectedness of things is experienced as something palpable. "It's like I can see the farm the pig lived on, and feel the sun and the rain on my face, and even taste the earth that the herbs grew out of," she reports.[13] One reason V is so popular is that it turns its users on to what they believe is a truer perception of reality, in which everything is experienced as connected and sensation is heightened beyond belief. This experience, which Amy Burley calls "the deepest connection to Gaia," is, in her opinion, divine. "This is what Holy Communion is symbolic of," she tells Jason Stackhouse as they dose themselves. "This is the real deal."[14] If only a drop or two of vampire blood can awaken a human being to an experience of divine transcendence, we can only imagine the everyday experience of vampires with gallons of the stuff coursing through their veins.

In short, the assumption that human beings occupy the highest rung on the great ladder of being is challenged in the world of *True Blood* by the existence of a species that seems to be superior to us in every way, possibly even in their kinship with the divine. If, as many philosophers have argued, human "dignity" derives from our transcendence of the limitations of "mere nature," then these *immortal*, almost godlike beings have us beat in that category as well. In our world, human beings are at the top of the food chain. Our rational abilities have put us far ahead of all the other animals, and for thousands of years we have been the dominant species. But in *True Blood*, we're number two. We have to wonder why vampires would seek equality with human beings in the first place. Equality seems like it would be quite a step down.

But perhaps we can still claim a *moral* superiority to vampires. After all, according to Kant, it's not just any old cognitive talent that elevated us above every other creature. It's our ability to recognize our moral obligations to other rational beings like ourselves and to allow morality, rather than wanton appetites and desires, to guide our conduct. It's that capacity for moral autonomy that makes us genuine *persons*, deserving of respect, as opposed to mere *things* that can be treated any which way we please. The Fellowship of the Sun's wholesale rejection of rights for vampires rests in large part on their belief that whatever else these creatures might be, they certainly aren't persons capable of moral conduct. The issue comes up when Jason informs Sarah Newlin that he knew a vampire named Eddie whom Jason believed was "a real nice person." Sarah corrects him. "He wasn't a person," she claims, since a person would never do something so foul as feeding on a human being.[15] (As she speaks, she gestures toward Missy, a recovering fang-banger whose neck and chest are dotted with bite marks.) Vampires may have abilities that surpass those of ordinary mortals, but, in Sarah's view, they lack something vital to personhood, the capacity to exercise moral judgment and restraint. They're not just inferior; they're *evil*.

But what exactly makes vampires evil? According to Sarah and the Fellowship it's that they feed on and exploit other creatures whom they, with some justification, regard as inferior beings—the very thing that Aristotle, Aquinas, and Kant all agree we *human beings* are entitled to do, as long as we're exploiting animals that occupy a rung lower than ours on the ladder of being. The allegedly evil actions of vampires differ not one scintilla from what we ourselves do all the time to our fellow creatures who suffer the misfortune of not being human. If our superiority grants us the right to exploit creatures further down the food chain from ourselves, why shouldn't vampires enjoy the same privilege?

When Bill stakes Longshadow in order to save Sookie, he commits a serious crime in the eyes of the vampire community, comparable to a human being committing a homicide to protect a nonhuman animal. "You murdered a higher life form for the sake of your pet," the magister fulminates in a tone of profound moral outrage.[16] Those are not the words of someone who lacks any sense of justice or moral propriety. On the contrary, they express a moral outlook that isn't significantly different from that of most human beings, except that we prefer to think of the "higher life forms" as ourselves.

Human Pets and Cattle

Most vampires on *True Blood* are just as guilty of speciesism as human beings, having no problem treating human beings as a means to an end. Lorena puts it quite succinctly to Bill: "You are vampire. They are *food*."[17] On other occasions, vampires describe human beings as animals. "You and your insane affection for stupid cattle," quips Pam when Bill expresses concern for Jessica.[18] Lorena and Pam are both disdainful of Bill's insistence on treating humans as equals. "Humans exist to serve us, that is their only value," says the magister at Bill's trial, using words that sound suspiciously like the way Aristotle, Aquinas, and Kant describe the value of nonhuman animals.[19] And like animals in our society, human beings can serve vampires in one of two ways—as food or as pets.

"I was hoping I could keep you," Pam tells Lafayette, as if he were a stray puppy, before releasing him from wretched captivity at Fangtasia. "You already have enough pets," scoffs Eric Northman.[20] The politically correct term for a human being kept by a vampire for food, sex, and company is "human companion," but to vampires, these human beings are usually little more than playthings to be possessed and exchanged. Vampires tend to think of their human companions in pretty much the same way we regard our pets—as useful, amusing, and even loveable, but never as equals. Ultimately, human beings are *property*. "Sookie is mine!" Bill routinely growls anytime another vampire looks at her the wrong way—and this assertion of a proprietary claim usually does this trick, since, as we saw with the magister, vampires do have their own clearly defined sense of justice in their dealings with one another.

Eric presents a threat to Bill because he wants Sookie for himself, seeing her as a special kind of pet whose telepathic skills identify her as a member of a more select "breed" than run-of-the-mill humans. He asks that Bill "give" her to him as though she were a mere object.[21] Sookie is understandably offended by Eric's suggestion. "He cannot check me out like a library book!" she protests when Bill allows Eric to "borrow" her. "Unfortunately, he can," Bill explains.[22] Ultimately, Bill is right. Vampires are powerful beings who can exert their dominion over human beings even more easily than we can over nonhuman animals.

Pam calls human beings "pathetic lumps of temporary flesh," apparently reflecting the attitude of most vampires, who view our species with pity and contempt because of our relatively impoverished experience of life.[23] To turn a human being into a vampire is to give her "the ultimate gift," freeing her from the unbearable tedium of mortal experience and raising her to a higher level of consciousness. The human experience of the world is so far below that of vampires that many vampires consider human beings to be almost insensate by comparison. "Humans are quite primitive," says the magister at Bill's tribunal. "They are incapable of feeling pain as we do"—which is apparently what gives vampires permission to treat human beings however they please without any moral qualms.[24] A similar—and equally unwarranted—skepticism about the reality of animal pain had been used by the philosopher René Descartes (1596–1650) to justify the barbaric practice of vivisection, the dissection of live, unanesthetized animals to study the workings of their internal organs.[25]

We are right to feel indignant, even outraged, at the magister's words, but we shouldn't lose sight of the fact that his attitude is really no different from the way many of us regard nonhuman animals. There's no question that our rational capacities put us at a level far beyond most other species, and many of us take this to mean that these other animals should be treated as inferior beings with no rights we're obliged to respect. Some people, such as Descartes, have even convinced themselves that nonhuman animals cannot feel pain or that their experiences are so narrow that killing these beings doesn't even count as taking a life. Jessica, whom Pam calls a "cow," is killed as part of a creative punishment designed for Bill, her death considered morally meaningless in itself simply because she's human. As Jessica pleads for mercy at the hands of a mob of indifferent vampires, we can't help but feel the injustice of her fate. Why should a vampire get to decide whether Jessica dies, when her life is obviously as precious to her as any vampire's existence is to him, despite her more "primitive" cognitive and sensory abilities? But to the vampires, Jessica's death means nothing. It is morally irrelevant because she belongs to an inferior species. And to millions of people around the world, the deaths of nonhuman animals mean nothing for this very same reason.

Our Civic Duty

The AVL prefers to make its case for vampire rights by highlighting how "human" vampires are or at least *were*, suggesting that they therefore ought to be granted human rights. But Nan Flanagan's letter to supporters on the AVL Web site actually describes the aim of her organization in much broader terms, referring to "the passage of landmark legislation guaranteeing a basic set of rights for all sentient beings."[26] As a qualification for moral consideration, sentience is very different from the possession of rationality, a moral sense, or a deep and rich experience of the world. The latter are all *powers* that many believe ought to command our respect when we encounter them in other beings. Sentience, on the other hand, is not only a power but, more importantly, a point of vulnerability, our exposure to the possibility of suffering. To make sentience the criterion for moral consideration amounts to replacing the question "What can you *do* that might warrant my respect?" with the question "How might you be *harmed* by my actions or neglect?" Or as the English philosopher Jeremy Bentham

(1748–1832) put it, referring to our duties to nonhuman animals, "[T]he question is not, Can they *reason*? nor, Can they *talk*? but, Can they *suffer*?"[27] If they can suffer, then what I do to them matters. It matters to them, obviously, but it should also matter to me.

When Bill asks Sookie why she came to his aid when the Rattrays were attacking him, she answers simply, "I was doing my civic duty."[28] Generally speaking, there are two attitudes we can take toward animals and those who are more vulnerable than us—we can exploit their vulnerability and use them to suit our own needs or we can see their vulnerability as a call to protect them from unnecessary harm. Sookie's attitude toward Bill represents the latter view, Denise and Mack Rattray's the former. When it comes to the treatment of vulnerable human beings, almost everyone will acknowledge that Sookie's attitude is more compassionate and virtuous. But is it really our civic duty to protect and respect members of *other* species just as Sookie protects Bill? Our response is to turn the question around and ask whether there is any valid reason to *exclude* members of other species from moral consideration. Basing their arguments on our species' supposedly superior cognitive talents and capacity for a high quality of life, many philosophers have tried to make a case for restricting our moral concern to human beings. But *True Blood* reveals how self-serving and questionable those arguments really are when it shows vampires reasoning along the same lines to justify the slaughter and exploitation of the species *they* regard as inferior—us. *True Blood* lets us see what it would be like to be a member of an exploited species. In so doing, it asks us to reexamine our prejudices about what constitutes the value of a living creature and perhaps reconsider whether our "civic duties" might reach beyond the boundaries of our own species.

Of course, if we conclude that all creatures, human or otherwise, have some inherent *dignity*, not just a market *price*, we then face tough questions about what should go on our dinner plates and in our clothes closets. No one can make those decisions for you. But if Bill Compton can get by on TruBlood, it probably wouldn't kill any of us to try a veggie burger.

NOTES

1. Episode 101, "Strange Love."

2. The American Vampire League Web site, www.americanvampireleague.com/about/index.html, accessed on January 22, 2010.

3. Episode 103, "Mine."

4. Here's how the philosopher Bertrand Russell (1872–1970) is reported to have responded to this claim: "It has been said that man is a rational animal. All my life I have been searching for evidence which could support this."

5. Aristotle, *The Politics and the Constitution of Athens*, trans. Stephen Everson (Cambridge, UK: Cambridge Univ. Press, 1996), p. 21 (1256b).

6. Thomas Aquinas, *Summa Theologica*, vol. 2, trans. Fathers of the English Dominican Province (Allen, TX: Christian Classics), 1981, p. 1080 (II, I, Q. 102, Art. 6).

7. Immanuel Kant, *Groundwork of the Metaphysics of Morals*, trans. Mary Gregor (Cambridge, UK: Cambridge Univ. Press, 1998), p. 42.

8. Episode 105, "Sparks Fly Out."

9. Episode 101, "Strange Love."

10. For a deeply disturbing account of how animals are treated on factory farms, see "Down on the Factory Farm," chapter 3 of Peter Singer's *Animal Liberation*, updated ed. (New York: HarperCollins, 2009), pp. 95–157.

11. For a philosophical examination of how human language and reason are rooted in cognitive abilities we share with other animals, see Alasdair MacIntyre's *Dependent Rational Animals: Why Human Beings Need the Virtues* (La Salle, IL: Open Court, 2001), especially pp. 1–61. For an exploration of the origins of human morality in the sense of fairness and empathy displayed by nonhuman primates, see Frans De Waal's Tanner Lectures, *Primates and Philosophers: How Morality Evolved* (Princeton, NJ: Princeton Univ. Press, 2009).

12. Singer, *Animal Liberation*, p. 20.

13. Episode 102, "The First Taste."

14. Episode 107, "Burning House of Love."

15. Episode 203, "Scratches."

16. Episode 110, "I Don't Wanna Know."

17. Episode 206, "The Hard-Hearted Hanna."

18. Episode 111, "To Love Is to Bury."

19. Episode 110, "I Don't Wanna Know."

20. Episode 203, "Scratches."

21. Episode 112, "You'll Be the Death of Me."

22. Episode 108, "The Fourth Man in the Fire."

23. Episode 111, "To Love Is to Bury."

24. Ibid.

25. For René Descartes' skepticism about animal sensation, see his *Discourse on Method*, trans. Donald Cress (Indianapolis: Hackett Publishing, 1998), pp. 32–33; and *The Philosophical Writings of Descartes, Vol. 3: The Correspondence*, trans. John Cottingham, Robert Stoothoff, Dugald Murdoch, and Anthony Kenny (Cambridge, UK: Cambridge Univ. Press, 1991), pp. 99–100.

26. The American Vampire League Web site, www.americanvampireleague.com/about/index.html, accessed on January 22, 2010.

27. Jeremy Bentham, *The Principles of Morals and Legislation* (Amherst, NY: Prometheus Books, 1988), p. 311.

28. Episode 102, "The First Taste."

PART TWO

"LIFE-CHALLENGED INDIVIDUALS": THE POLITICS OF BEING DEAD

SIGNED IN BLOOD

Rights and the Vampire-Human Social Contract

Joseph J. Foy

With the advent of synthetic blood produced by the Yakonomo Corporation, vampires decided it was safe to reveal their existence to the human world. According to Tiffany McElroy, a broadcast journalist in the mockumentary *In Focus: Vampires in America*, the so-called Great Revelation forced humanity to "reexamine every notion we've ever had about life, the natural world, and even our own existence."[1] And while men and women everywhere were reconsidering what it meant to be a member of the human race, the Great Revelation also raised an intriguing political question: Do vampires deserve rights?

Even more overtly than Charlaine Harris in her Southern Vampire Mysteries, Alan Ball uses *True Blood* to explore the questions the Great Revelation raises regarding equality, justice, and civil rights in a democratic society. Tapping into contemporary debates about diversity, gender, identity politics, and immigration, *True Blood* offers important philosophical insights about justice and the proper role of the state in establishing and protecting rights.

We're Here. We're Dead. Get Over It.

In a televised address to the United States as part of the Great Revelation, an unnamed vampire stood in front of the American flag claiming that "all we [vampires] want is to coexist with you [human beings] and enjoy the same rights and freedoms as everyone else."[2] Advocates for vampire rights like Nan Flanagan, spokesperson for the American Vampire League (AVL), echo these sentiments. In an interview on *Real Time with Bill Maher*, Nan asserts, "We're citizens. We pay taxes. We deserve basic civil rights just like everyone else."[3] Vampires are seeking the equal protection of the state *in exchange* for their adherence to the basic laws and norms of society.

Implied within Nan's statement is a traditional view of the state as having been formed by a social contract. A social contract is an agreement between individuals, or between citizens and their government, that establishes and underwrites the laws that govern society. Under such a contract, individuals consent to enforceable limits on their actions *in exchange* for rights and protections provided by the state. Nan maintains that because vampires participate fully in the civic obligations asked of any citizen—respecting the law and paying taxes—they deserve to be treated as equal partners in the social contract alongside human beings.

In order to promote vampire rights, the AVL actively lobbies in support of the Vampire Rights Amendment (VRA), a bill that, if passed, would provide a guarantee that equal protection under the law will not be denied to any individual on the basis of being a vampire. The VRA would provide constitutional recognition of vampires, allowing them to file suit against public acts of discrimination. It would shield vampires from attempts to infringe on their social, political, and economic rights.

The VRA is not without its critics, however. Spearheaded by the Fellowship of the Sun, opponents of vampire rights offer numerous arguments to discredit the notion that vampires deserve equal protection. For example, Reverend Theodore Newlin, leader of the Fellowship, appears on a TBBN news program to argue that the state should never have granted vampires basic political rights, such as the right to vote, because it "legitimized their unholy existence." Claiming that vampires are "creatures of Satan" and a demonic presence, Newlin insists that principles of political equality should not apply to vampires because they "have no soul."[4]

The contrasting perspectives of the AVL and the Fellowship of the Sun, while fictional, have a familiar ring. Contemporary American society is filled with clashes between minority and majority groups (divided by race, gender, and sexual orientation), religious and secular communities (divided over issues like the teaching of evolution in public schools and public displays of religious artifacts), and different interpretations of the obligations the state has to its citizens. These debates are unavoidable in a liberal republic like the United States, a regime that protects individual rights and in which citizens actively participate in government through the election of representatives. What makes the Great Revelation so interesting is that it creates a compelling test of social contract theory and gives us a new perspective on the demands of diversity in democratic society.

This American "Un-Life"

For a small Louisiana town, Bon Temps has a vibrantly diverse population. It has its religious and secular communities, public employees and business owners, and a host of unique individuals who represent different elements of American life. In Bon Temps we meet Sookie Stackhouse, a telepathic, single waitress; her grandmother Adele Stackhouse, whose greatest joy seems to come from learning about local history at her Descendants of the Glorious Dead meetings; Sookie's handsome, blue-collar, womanizing brother, Jason; Sam Merlotte, owner of the popular bar and grill; Tara Thornton, a strong-willed African American woman who is quick to confront anyone in whom she senses even a hint of racism or sexism; her cousin Lafayette Reynolds, an openly gay short-order cook whom we would expect to find in a more urban environment than Bon Temps; and Arlene Fowler, a single mother in an on-again-off-again relationship with a man who currently goes by the name Rene Lenier. And when Bill Compton walks into Merlotte's, Bon Temps "welcomes" its first vampire.

The cast of characters that makes Bon Temps unique is also what makes it typically American. It's a community of individuals all trying to carve out a space for themselves in which to pursue the things that make them happy. The United States was formed largely out of groups of people as diverse as this collection of Bon Temp residents, all of whom agreed to establish a government that didn't impose a uniform way of life upon its citizens. Borrowing from the political philosophy of John Locke (1632–1704), the American founders established a regime that protects individual rights and allows citizens to pursue their own happiness so long as they don't trample on the "life, liberty, health, limb, or goods of another."[5] Sookie can fall in love with a vampire, Jason can date an assortment of women, and Lafayette can, well, be Lafayette. All are free to pursue happiness in their own ways as long as they don't hurt anyone else.

That's not to say that the United States has always lived up to its founding promises. As Tara is quick to remind everyone, America's legacy of slavery and its ongoing problems of race and gender discrimination fly in the face of the values of liberty, equality, and democracy. Ideally, though, ours is a pluralistic society, with tolerance for diversity and a commitment to individual rights. According to our pluralistic ideals, you're free to express yourself openly and practice your chosen faith without having to subscribe to a particular set of officially sanctioned beliefs. Moreover, you can enjoy the rights of a citizen without having to belong to a particular race, gender, class, or (in the case of vampires) "life-or-death-hood." As long as your actions don't directly impose on others, the state should leave you alone.

The advent of the synthetic TruBlood (called TrueBlood in the Southern Vampire Mysteries) makes it possible to expand the concept of pluralism to include vampires. As Nan explained to Bill Maher, after he challenged her to consider the historical legacy of vampires feeding on and exploiting humans, "Now that the Japanese have perfected synthetic blood, which satisfies all our nutritional needs, there is no need for anyone to fear us."[6] It's because of the development of synthetic blood that vampires decided to make their existence known. No longer needing to prey on human beings, vampires can "mainstream" into human society. Everyone can live and let un-live.

A Vampire's Right to Life?

Locke's natural rights philosophy provides the basis for the equal protection of life, liberty, and property for *human* beings, but does it really support the incorporation of *vampires* into civil society? Even apart from the obvious paradox of enforcing a right to life for someone who's already dead, the claim that vampires have natural rights runs up against the belief of groups like the Fellowship of the Sun (probably shared by many ordinary citizens) that vampires are not endowed with any natural rights because their very existence is *unnatural*.

The Reverend Newlin puts forward just such a notion. From his perspective, God could not have endowed vampires with the same natural rights as human beings because vampires are not really God's creations at all. In an interview on the TV network TBBN, Newlin says of vampires, "Literally, they have no soul." Lacking a soul, vampires can be denied the basic rights of human beings. Newlin suggests that vampires are a perversion of nature to whom natural rights need not apply. His perspective recalls actual historical arguments suggesting that members of certain racial minorities are not fully human, which led to laws depriving them of rights on the basis of skin color (and even enslaving them). By the same token, the argument that vampires cannot be granted the same rights as human beings because they're "unnatural" calls to mind claims used to oppose legal recognition for same-sex unions.

Of course, Nan Flanagan and other members of the AVL attempt to counter the claims that their existence is unnatural. "Who's to say what's natural? Who's to say that what my body can do is any less natural than what yours can do?" asks Nan in her *In Focus* interview. Statements about naturalness are matters of perspective, faith, and belief—not empirical claims that can be demonstrated with any certainty.[7] But in the theory of John Locke, *rights* are natural, not merely established by law or the social contract. The social contract is merely our agreement to submit to a common authority that exists solely to enforce and protect the rights we already possess by nature. So from a Lockean perspective, where does that leave our theory of the state in terms of its obligations to citizens whose bodies never grow warmer than room temperature?

It's clear that the state must do something to avoid extreme lawlessness. From the moment Bill arrives in Bon Temps, we witness the problems that would prevail if the state didn't establish and maintain equal rights. Mack and Denise Rattray are among a growing class of criminals who sell vampire blood (or V). Their attempt to drain Bill outside of Merlotte's Bar and Grill is foiled by Sookie, who is herself attacked by the Rattrays later when they come back bent on revenge. The brutal murder of fang-bangers by Rene Lenier (or, as he was known in the nearby town of Bunkie, Drew Marshall); the vigilante torching of the home of Liam, Diane, and Malcolm; Eric's murder of Royce (one of the arsonists); and Steve Newlin's attempt to initiate a war against the vampires to satisfy his quest for vengeance after the death of his father—all are the kinds of violent acts that should invoke the protection of the state. If vampires were given no legal status to guarantee this protection, we would undoubtedly see even more and worse cases of this sort of violence.

But it's not just police protections we expect from the state. We also count on the state for protection against unjust discrimination, whether by government agencies or private businesses. A news broadcast on TBBN reminds us of one of those important protections when it announces that the Vermont Supreme Court overturned laws restricting human-vampire marriage, finding them to be an unconstitutional violation of equal protection.[8] We're also reminded of these protections by the title sequence of each episode of *True Blood*, which includes historical images of the struggle of African Americans in the civil rights movement for the right to be fully enfranchised and to participate at all levels of the social, economic, and political life of their nation. It was the Fourteenth Amendment's "equal protection clause"—stating that equal protection under the law cannot be denied to any born or naturalized citizen—that allowed African Americans and other minorities to seek help from the courts to overcome discrimination and gain equal access to housing, voting, employment, education, and public accommodations. Vampires face similar discrimination after the Great Revelation, at least to some extent. As Bill plans the renovations he wants to make on his newly inherited home, Sookie reminds him that the property is legally his only if the VRA passes. It's not enough for the state to protect people from harm. It must also ensure equal access and opportunity for all people, so they can be fully included within the social contract that underlies civil society.

The Great Fanged Menace

Of course, one could argue that because vampires have a history of feeding on people—however valiantly Nan attempts to gloss over that bit of history by claiming that there's no historical record of violence—vampires are not deserving of rights. But the AVL can counter that human beings too have a record of abuse and inhumane acts, including slavery, dropping an atomic bomb on civilian populations, thousands of years of war, and, in just the last century, genocide on an unprecedented scale. A history of violence can't be used as the basis for a blanket denial of political rights unless we're prepared to disenfranchise ourselves as well.

Fear of rogue vampires, who assert predatory superiority over human beings and refuse to feed on synthetic blood, causes skepticism and hatred of all vampires by some human beings. *True Blood* provides evidence that there are quite a few rogues roaming around—after all, the assassination of Theodore Newlin by rogue vampires is what led to his son Steve's taking over the Fellowship of the Sun. But even if not all vampires want to mainstream, this isn't a good reason to deny equal rights to vampires as a group. Many human beings are dangerous—the Rattrays and Rene come to mind—but the actions of a few lawbreakers don't justify restricting the rights of everyone else. Moreover, groups like the Fellowship of the Sun pose just as serious a threat to the vampire community as rogue vampires do to human beings. The Fellowship's plan to make all vampires "greet the sun" aims at a vampire holocaust. And the paramilitary training of the Soldiers of the Sun, an elite group of vampire hunters who serve the Fellowship, shows that they mean to deliver on their threats. As Steve's bumper sticker announces, the Fellowship wants to take the "un" out of "undead."

Just as we can't strip all human beings of their political rights because of the danger posed by a few, it would be misguided and wrong to do that to vampires. The Lockean theory of the state would demand the equal protection of vampire rights *if*, of course, vampires really possessed any rights by nature. But what exactly entitles someone to rights, and how do we know who has them?

Locke argued that since God created us, we are in effect God's property. God wants us to live, and we therefore have a right not only to go on living, but to retain our liberty and property, which Locke thought were necessary for our survival. Our duties to others are derived from our obligation to protect God's property. But is belief in God necessary in order to be admitted to the social contract that protects our God-given rights? Locke suggests that it is, going so far as to claim that "those are not at all to be tolerated who deny the being of God" because "promises, covenants, and oaths, which are the bond of human society, can have no hold upon an atheist."[9] Since Locke's political philosophy of toleration extends only to those who believe in God, it is legitimate from his perspective to withhold full legal protection from those who in all other respects adhere to the civil law of the state.

Moreover, Locke simply assumes that human beings are the *only* creatures whom God endowed with rights. But can we really fault him for not anticipating vampires' coming out of the coffin and insisting that they *too* have rights that society should recognize?

Vampires Were People, Too

Given the problems the Great Revelation poses for Locke's view of natural rights and the state, we might want to look to alternative ways of understanding where rights come from and how they must be upheld. One such view was proposed by John Rawls (1921–2002), who, like Locke, believed that rights exist prior to the establishment of the state, which comes into being through a social contract designed to protect those rights. However, unlike Locke, Rawls did not couch his theory in terms of God-given rights in a state of nature. Consequently, Rawls offered a theory that allows for greater toleration and diversity within a democratic society. Famously, Rawls proposed a thought experiment involving what he called "the original position," showing how it would be possible for a group of rational deliberators to arrive at a consensus concerning the social contract, without appealing to divisive theories about natural or divine rights.[10]

Imagine a group of individuals—not just human beings but also vampires, shapeshifters, Weres, fairies, maenads, and perhaps other creatures that are capable of entering into rational deliberation. Stand them outside of any existing society and ask them to choose from a host of political alternatives the structure of the society under which they will live together. Imagine also that they're completely ignorant of their own personal characteristics—their race, class, gender, religion, species, and social and historical circumstances—although they do have some general understanding of biology, psychology, economics, politics, and other subjects. Most important, assume that they're rational beings capable of understanding the consequences of their decisions behind this hypothetical "veil of ignorance." What social arrangements would they choose in such conditions?

Rawls believes that if a group of individuals entered into a social contract under these circumstances, with no knowledge of their own personal fortunes to bias their considerations in favor of their own group, they would all choose a society that, first and foremost, provides basic civil rights and freedoms for each individual equally. This would allow for a society in which all of the parties to this contract would be able to peacefully coexist and pursue the good life regardless of whom or *what* they are, provided of course they respect the rights of others. If anti-vampire zealots like the Newlins were forced to deliberate about justice behind Rawls's veil of ignorance, not knowing if they might themselves thirst for a platelet-filled liquid diet, their anti-vampire bigotry couldn't influence their decisions about the distribution of basic rights and social goods. Likewise, vampires like Liam, Diane, and Malcolm wouldn't be so willing to consider vampire supremacy a foregone conclusion if, for all they knew, they could end up as mortal as their prey.

According to a Lockean view, the state exists only to protect our basic natural rights to things like life, liberty, and property. The Rawlsian social contract, on the other hand, is also concerned with distributive justice, the question of how to allocate fairly the benefits and burdens of living in society. One of the principles that Rawls believes the parties to the social contract would agree to in the "original position" is that "all social values—liberty and opportunity, income and wealth, and the bases of self-respect—are to be distributed equally unless an unequal distribution of any or all of these is to everyone's advantage."[11] Inequality of *outcome* in society is justifiable as long as everyone has equality of *opportunity* and, moreover, as long as social inequalities work to everyone's advantage, especially those at the bottom of society. For example, we can justify paying a doctor more than a ditch digger, since the extra compensation will attract the most qualified people to the medical profession, something from which we all benefit. Rawls's principles of justice are designed to extend fairness and recognition to everyone, especially to those who would otherwise fall through the cracks. For as Tara tells Jason when they're sitting alone on the couch in Adele's living room, "Everybody is, you know, somebody. . . . We're all just trying to be seen, to matter."[12] Consequently, deliberators behind the veil of ignorance would favor social arrangements that treat every person as though he or she *does* matter. For example, Rawls believes that a just state would provide everyone with fair and equal access to basic social resources like education, employment, and participation in the political process.

When it comes to the distribution of economic resources, Rawls's principles of justice might very well work to the advantage of human beings. Vampires like Eric Northman and Bill (let alone Godric) have had centuries to accumulate private wealth that gives them a substantial economic advantage over mortals. Given the power, influence, and access to other resources that comes with wealth, this disparity could lead to what Rawls considers an unjust outcome, namely, an extreme inequality that is in no way beneficial to the least advantaged, in this case, human beings. Rawls's theory of justice forces us to reexamine how society deals with the advantages derived from accumulated wealth. Behind the veil of ignorance, rational deliberators might choose to institute a system that allows vampires and mortals alike to accumulate private property and will it to others, but it's also likely that they would want the government to redistribute some of that wealth through progressive taxation and providing social services to the needy. While Rawls still defends classically liberal notions of capitalism and private property, his theory of justice also allows for a progressive redistribution of wealth that ensures a social safety net and extends to everyone the opportunity to succeed. Such principles of distributive justice are absent from the social contract theory of John Locke.

Rawls focuses on how to secure the basic liberties and opportunities that will allow all citizens to participate fully in the social, political, and economic life of a diverse society. For Rawls, the validity of the social contract doesn't depend on our sharing any belief about God. All the Rawlsian contract demands of us is that we possess the capacity for reason. If vampires are just as capable as human beings of rational thought (and there is significant evidence on *True Blood* that they are), then they can be equal partners in the social contract. Reason would order society, securing equal liberty for all, while ensuring a distribution of resources that benefits even the least advantaged in society. In some cases, that distribution might benefit human beings, while in other cases it might benefit vampires. In no way, however, could reason lead us to establish a society based on unfairly denying basic rights to any group or individual. If our diverse human population can construct a just society using the Rawlsian thought experiment of the original position, there's no reason that vampires can't be party to that contract. For all that matters is the rational exercise of the mind, not the beating pulse of the heart or God's granting of a soul, when formulating the principles of a just society.

On Coffins and Contracts

Although Alan Ball's *True Blood* explicitly deals with the political challenges vampirism poses for human society, it's in Charlaine Harris's Southern Vampire Mysteries that we find the best example of a justification for political rights based on rational deliberation. In *Dead until Dark*, Sookie does not kill Rene Lenier. Rather, she escapes and runs to Bill's house, where she telephones the authorities just before passing out. Bill comes to visit her in the hospital, the same hospital where Rene, now under arrest, is also recovering. Knowing Bill's desire for vengeance, Sookie tells him, "Don't kill Rene. . . . [T]here's been enough murder. Let the law do it. I don't want any more witch hunts coming after you. I want us to have peace."[13] Her request reflects the view that first and foremost, the state must protect everyone's rights equally to eliminate the problems caused by personal vengeance and private defense. Only then can we establish the peace necessary for a free society. But it's equally important to afford access to social goods in a manner that guarantees equal opportunity to all. As Ball demonstrates time and again in *True Blood*, the twofold goals of political equality and access to key social resources regardless of race, gender, sexuality, class, or "dietary needs" is the lifeblood of any social contract that could underwrite a pluralist democracy like that of the United States.[14]

NOTES

1. *In Focus: Vampires in America*, supplementary material on the DVD *True Blood: The Complete First Season*, Home Box Office Network, 2009.

2. Ibid.

3. Episode 101, "Strange Love."

4. Episode 102, "First Taste."

5. These are the rights, identified by Locke, that no one can be justly deprived of. See John Locke, *The Second Treatise of Government*, ed. Thomas P. Peardon (Indianapolis: Bobbs-Merrill, 1952), pp. 5–6.

6. Episode 101, "Strange Love."

7. For more on the problem of deciding what's "natural," see Andrew and Jenny Terjesen's chapter in this volume, "Are Vampires Unnatural?"

8. Episode 112, "You'll Be the Death of Me."

9. John Locke, *A Letter Concerning Toleration* (Indianapolis: Bobbs-Merrill, 1955), p. 52.

10. John Rawls first elaborated these ideas in *A Theory of Justice* (Cambridge, MA: Harvard Univ. Press, 1999).

11. Ibid., p. 54.

12. Episode 102, "The First Taste."

13. Charlaine Harris, *Dead until Dark* (New York: Ace Books, 2001), p. 291.

14. I would like to thank Dean A. Kowalski, Timothy M. Dale, and Rochelle Sack for their observations and suggestions while developing this essay, and George Dunn and Rebecca Housel for their comments and revisions. Thanks also to Margaret Hankenson for introducing me to *True Blood*, and to Kristi Nelson Foy for the Sookie Stackhouse novels.

"HONEY, IF WE CAN'T KILL PEOPLE, WHAT'S THE POINT OF BEING A VAMPIRE?"

Can Vampires Be Good Citizens?

William M. Curtis

Thanks to the Japanese invention of synthetic blood, vampires have "come out of the coffin" and are (ostensibly) attempting to "mainstream" by openly integrating into human society. This prospect presents innumerable political and legal complications unaddressed by *True Blood*. Should there be a Truth and Reconciliation Commission to require vamps to come clean about their past murders in return for a grant of amnesty? How should vampires be taxed, especially since they don't need many of the services that government provides, like Social Security, health care, and education? Can they join, or be drafted into, the armed forces? (Perhaps we can imagine them serving in elite, night-ops commando units, akin to, although hopefully more professional than, the Bloodpack in *Blade II*.) Will their vulnerability to sunlight be treated as a disability under the

Americans with Disabilities Act? Can vampire convicts be sentenced to life in prison, or would eternal incarceration violate the Eighth Amendment prohibition on cruel and unusual punishment? Should the Civil Rights Acts be amended to ban the use of garlic in restaurants?

While the *True Blood* audience is reasonably asked to suspend their consideration of these sorts of practical conundrums, the issue of vampire mainstreaming is still central to the series. It squarely confronts us with this question: Can vampires live up to the obligations of citizenship imposed by modern liberal democracy? The flip side of this question is this: How should a liberal political community deal with these vampire citizens?

As disappointing as it may be for would-be fang-bangers and vampire sympathizers, this chapter argues that it would be foolish for liberal human society to attempt to integrate the *True Blood* vampires. Integration of these vamps poses a unique political challenge, because they have long been participants in an illiberal, hierarchical political system that is incompatible with even the most tolerant philosophical conceptions of liberalism. Moreover, there isn't much evidence to suggest that these vampires want to become law-abiding citizens of our political community, or even that they can, given their nature.

Note that this chapter uses the term *liberal* in its historical, philosophical sense to mean a commitment to a basic range of human rights, like the sort found in the American Bill of Rights: freedom of speech, religion, and association, protection of property rights, freedom from arbitrary imprisonment, and so on. For our purposes, "liberal" does not refer, as it does in most current political conversation, to the platform of the left wing of the Democratic Party. (Thus, while it may strike one's ears as strange, in the sense of the term liberal used here, Rush Limbaugh and Dick Cheney are *liberals!*)

Liberal societies pride themselves on their toleration of ethical and cultural diversity. As the philosopher John Rawls (1921–2002) insisted, the point of a liberal political regime is to create "a stable and just society of free and equal citizens profoundly divided by reasonable but incompatible religious, philosophical, and moral doctrines."[1] Indeed, for the last couple of decades, the issue of relationship between liberalism and diversity has been *the* hot topic of liberal theory. A primary reason for this is that as our society continues to become more global, various minority and subculture groups are increasingly demanding that liberal society recognize and accommodate their unique cultural and religious practices. These demands sometimes involve claims for "group rights" or for exemptions from general laws that conflict with the groups' traditions. In the United States, for example, the Amish successfully petitioned the Supreme Court to exempt their children from a mandatory state schooling requirement.[2] In Great Britain, the turban-wearing Sikhs are exempt from motorcycle helmet laws (although in Ontario, Canada, they are not), while some Muslims campaign for official recognition of religious Sharia courts' jurisdiction over British Muslims. In France, Muslims insist that Muslim girls should be able to wear the head veil in schools, against national policy, and in the Netherlands, many annually flout anti-animal-cruelty laws on the holiday of Eid al-Adha by slaughtering sacrificial goats in their homes. The search for principles to guide liberal societies in determining which practices they can and cannot reasonably tolerate is one of the most pressing philosophical tasks of our time.

Vamp and Camp: Does Out of the Coffin = Out of the Closet?

The Great Revelation, of course, presents liberal society with yet another unique subculture that is claiming its civil rights. But are vampires just one more form of diversity that liberal society must tolerate and even accommodate in certain ways, or are vampires beyond the pale of liberal toleration? After all, they're not exactly the Amish! Yet liberalism does support equal rights for gays, and as the *True Blood* "coffin" metaphor suggests, the series implies at least some superficial similarities between the respective cultural situations of vampires and gays.[3] For example, vampires have always lived among us as a secret community and now have formed a public movement to ask the larger society to accept their kind and recognize their equal rights. As with the gay rights movement, vampires face generalized, pervasive anti-vampire prejudice as well as organized opposition, particularly in the form of the militant Christian evangelical group called the Fellowship of the Sun. Indeed, *True Blood* creator Alan Ball has commented that the police raid on the Shreveport vampire bar, Fangtasia, in the fourth episode of season 1, "Escape from the Dragon House," was meant to resemble similar raids on gay bars in the 1960s.[4] The events of the next episode are also telling. After Bill Compton and Sookie Stackhouse flee from the Fangtasia raid, they are pulled over by a cop. Bill becomes so indignant and fierce that Sookie is afraid that he will kill the officer, but Bill only "glamours" him, takes his gun, threatens him, and leaves him peeing his pants. Afterward, Bill comments, "We've had a difficult relationship with law enforcement for many years."[5] Vampires are presented here as a classic oppressed minority that liberal society must recognize and tolerate if it is to live up to its ideal of justice.

On the other hand, the gay/vampire analogy goes only so far. After all, even before gays started coming out and gaining public visibility, it is safe to say that most people at least knew of their existence (even homophobes, who wished they didn't exist). Before the Great Revelation, however, most people believed that vampires were purely mythical monsters. The growing acceptance of gays in liberal society is celebrated by liberals and is painful for antigay bigots, but adjusting to the Great Revelation requires a cognitive adjustment of a higher order of magnitude. Moreover, there is the delicate matter that, as Bill emphatically insists to Sookie, vampires are not human but are instead supernatural undead who have a long history of killing humans for food and even sport. While some people view homosexuality as a moral and spiritual threat to society, vampires, as ravenous, superhuman serial killers, have indisputably been a physical threat to human beings. Nevertheless, now that vampires no longer need to feed on humans, the American Vampire League (AVL) insists that they can become upstanding members of liberal society. But is this true?

It's Utterly Feudal: Reconciling Vampire Politics and Liberalism

There are at least a couple of formidable hurdles to recognizing vampires' rights and granting them equal citizenship. Although we can agree with Aristotle (384–322 B.C.E.) that ethics and politics are ultimately the same subject, we can usefully distinguish between two hurdles by calling them the *political problem* and the *ethical problem*. The political problem is somewhat unique to the *True Blood* universe. Although other vampire tales have portrayed hierarchical relationships among vampires, usually based on age or "bloodline," *True Blood* exhibits a more developed vampire political system. The problem is whether the vampire political system is compatible with the human liberal political order that the vampires aspire to join, or whether liberalism requires this system to be drastically modified or dismantled. The ethical problem presents the more fundamental question of whether vampires, by their nature, can really reform and become good, law-abiding members of society.

The vampire political system in *True Blood* is mysterious, to say the least. Although Charlaine Harris's Southern Vampire Mysteries provide a few more details than *True Blood* has thus far, we still don't know precisely how the system works or the exact nature of its authority. Nevertheless, here's what we can glean. The vampire political system in *True Blood* is feudal in nature. In America, every state appears to have a king or queen who rules with apparently absolute authority over the state's vampire population.[6] Sophie-Anne LeClerq, for example, is queen of Louisiana. States are divided into areas, once called fiefdoms, that are ruled by vampire sheriffs who owe allegiance to their state monarch. Louisiana is divided into five areas, and Eric Northman is sheriff of Area 5, which includes Bon Temps and Shreveport. Since Bill has taken up residence in Bon Temps, he must obey Eric, who in turn must obey Sophie-Anne. Sheriffs also retain several vampire henchmen, whom Harris refers to as lieutenants in her novels, although this term appears to be metaphorical rather than an official rank and title.

Toward the end of season 1 of *True Blood* we're introduced to yet another powerful vampire official: the magister, a judge who presides over a vampire tribunal that tries vampires and metes out punishment to them for breaking the ancient vampire laws.[7] Last, there's Nan Flanagan, the spokesvampire for the AVL, who berates the sheriff of Texas Area 9, the very old and powerful Godric, for allowing himself to be kidnapped by the Fellowship, for his subordinate Stan's raid on the the Fellowship's church, and for Luke's suicide bombing of Godric's lair.[8] She tells him, Trump-like, that he is "fired," though it's unclear whether she officially has that authority. Eric indicates that she doesn't, and her response is that she has the power because she is "on TV." He also calls her a "bureaucrat." Is her "bureaucracy" the AVL? What authority does it have? Nan refers to "higher-ups" who are unhappy about the public relations mess that Godric has created. But who are these higher-ups? State monarchs or some other as yet undisclosed level or branch of vampire hierarchy? It seems reasonable to assume, at least, that state monarchs have the power to appoint and remove their sheriffs. But how did the monarchs themselves come into power? It's not simply a matter of age. After all, Godric is the oldest vampire in North America, yet he's only a sheriff. In the Southern Vampire Mysteries, there are (temporary) marriages between, as well as wars of conquest among, vampire royalty, all of which further complicates vampire politics.

Already, one might suspect that this setup will be difficult for a liberal society to absorb, and yet the skeletal political structure just described doesn't even account for the strong, apparently supernatural, hold of obedience that vampire "makers" have over their "children," or the mysterious "blood bond" that is formed between a vampire and a human who have consumed one another's blood. Both of these relationships have the potential to usurp the autonomy of individuals in disturbing ways. Can these absolutist, illiberal political relationships be reconciled with a liberal political order?

The problem of vampire political life opens up a hotly debated question in contemporary liberal political philosophy: is liberalism primarily about promoting individual autonomy or tolerating diversity, including at least some nonliberal diversity? Generally speaking, *autonomy* refers to the capacity to freely and reflectively run one's own life. Liberal theorists who maintain that good liberal citizenship requires autonomy will be unable to accept the illiberal vampire political system and its culture of obedience. Stephen Macedo, for example, argues that good liberal citizens require a set of "liberal virtues," including "broad sympathies, self-critical reflection, a willingness to experiment, to try and accept new things, self-control and active, autonomous self-development, an appreciation of inherited social ideals, an attachment and even altruistic regard for one's fellow liberal citizens."[9] These virtues enable liberal citizens not only to participate in liberal politics aimed at creating a just set of laws and policies that treat all citizens as free and equal, but also to understand and abide by those laws and policies.

The *True Blood* vamps, however, don't generally exhibit these civic virtues. Perhaps they can be freely and creatively hedonistic, but the vampire subculture and hierarchy ultimately discourage the exercise of independence and autonomy. Even the defiant Bill, who seems closest to possessing liberal virtues, has no illusions about his place in the vampire pecking order. It doesn't seem to occur to him that mainstreaming might free him from obedience to Eric or Sophie-Anne. Moreover, the fact that even he doesn't hesitate to engage in brutal acts of vigilante justice, as when he kills the Rattrays and Uncle Bartlett, should also make us wonder whether vampires are ready for responsible citizenship. The liberal citizen's commitment to liberal justice must override all other value commitments; the vampire hierarchy cannot retain its authority if vampires are to legitimately join the human social contract.

But perhaps liberalism based on individual autonomy is too ethically demanding and oppresses what's distinctive about the vampire community. Many contemporary liberal philosophers argue that liberalism should not require autonomy and should instead tolerate and accommodate diverse communities that don't accept the value of autonomy. The philosopher Chandran Kukathas, for example, argues that the liberal state shouldn't interfere with the internal affairs of any subcommunity as long as that subcommunity doesn't physically coerce its members to remain a part of it.[10] Kukathas's liberalism emphasizes liberty of conscience and freedom of association rather than the moral ideal of autonomy. He's willing to tolerate any subcommunity no matter how illiberal or authoritarian its structure and practices as long as its members are technically free to leave (and even if the costs of leaving are very high). So if the *True Blood* vampires are free to disassociate themselves from the vampire political system, then human liberal society should tolerate it, just as it might tolerate a similarly oppressive religious cult. While it may be psychologically difficult for vampires to disengage themselves from relationship structures and habits of obedience that have been built up, in some cases, over centuries, this by itself is no reason for the liberal state to require the vampires to dismantle or even alter their political hierarchy. The liberal state, according to Kukathas, is merely a neutral umpire that preserves peaceful coexistence among an "archipelago" of different cultural communities. While it forbids the use of physical coercion within and among these communities, its role is not to impose a rigid conception of justice on society, nor to foster individual autonomy or any other ethical values among the citizenry.

But are the *True Blood* vampires free to leave their political system? What we witness in connection with the magister suggests otherwise. After sentencing one vampire to a bloody defanging, the magister then punishes Bill for killing the vampire Longshadow by forcing him to turn Jessica Hamby. We don't get the impression that vampires can simply choose to opt out of this system of "justice." That the magister holds court in a junkyard, out of the bed of what looks like a battered blue El Camino, suggests that the vampires are keen on keeping this whole illiberal feature of their culture secret from the human community they want to join. Moreover, this high vampire official expresses a chilling sentiment from the bench that should give us pause: "Humans exist to serve us. That is their *only* value." When Bill meekly dissents from this view, the magister harshly puts him in his place, reminding Bill that he is the vampire adjudicator for the whole of North America. The magister then sentences Bill to turn an innocent human girl whom the vampires have kidnapped for the occasion.[11]

We could surmise that the magister is a vestigial institution of the bad ol' days before the Great Revelation, soon to be stripped of authority by the enlightened "higher-ups" of the AVL. Yet during her scolding of Godric, Nan threatens to turn Godric, Eric, and others over to the magister, which suggests that the AVL acknowledges the legitimacy of the office (although perhaps the AVL is simply making use of it until it can be abolished). In any case, even in Kukathas's less demanding, more tolerant conception of liberalism, the vampire political system remains problematic: not only does it involve the physical coercion of vampires, it also mistreats humans with impunity. As it currently exists in the *True Blood* universe, the vampire political system cannot be tolerated by human liberal society.

What Is It Like to Be a Vampire?

While the details of the vampire political system are somewhat murky, one thing is clear: the vampires are in the midst of their own culture war. Although the invention of synthetic blood enabled the Great Revelation, it's unclear what motivated it or whose decision it was. There are vampires who want main-streaming to succeed, like Bill and Godric, and others who utterly disdain the project, like Malcolm and his mates. It's Malcolm's words ("Honey, if we can't kill people, what's the point of being a vampire?") that form the title of this chapter. He raises an interesting question: Could mainstreaming be contrary to vam-pire identity or, more fundamentally, against vampire nature? Malcolm's claim could mean that to be a "real" vampire, one must be a killer, and to peacefully integrate into human society is to destroy vampire identity. That's akin to claims made by some gay activists that to assimilate to heterosexual society (by, for example, entering into an institution like marriage that remains pretty traditional even when opened up to same-sex unions) is to renounce a more authentic gay identity. If enough vampires agree with Malcolm, human beings will be letting wolves into the fold if they invite vampires to participate with them as equals in society.

Still, Godric insists, and the AVL might agree, that vampires can "evolve" to live peacefully among humans, especially since as they age, they need less blood to survive. But we can't base our general assessment of the moral capacities of vampires on Godric, who is uniquely old and the only truly pacifist vampire we have yet met in *True Blood* (although perhaps the hapless, incompetent Eddie Gauthier also counts). The bottom line is that we ultimately don't know whether vampires are ethi-cally capable of obeying the laws and respecting the rights of their fellow citizens. Are we just going to take the AVL's word for it?

The title of this subsection alludes to a famous article by the philosopher Thomas Nagel titled "What Is It Like to Be a Bat?"[12] In his article, Nagel challenges reductionist theories of the mind such as the one that says once we've described the chemical processes of the brain, there's nothing left to say about the mind.[13] He points out that since bats are sentient, there is a subjective experience of what it is like to be a bat. This experience, however, is simply beyond human comprehension, because bats possess a radically different neurophysiology that, among other things, allows them to navigate the world through echolocation. Theories that reduce the mind to chemical processes in the brain, Nagel maintains, are unable to account for this sort of subjective experience and thus fail to explain this important feature of the mind. (The existence of shifters in the *True Blood* universe perhaps adds an interesting twist to Nagel's argument, although exploration of that will have to take place elsewhere.) Although Nagel merely hints at the ethical ramifications of dealing with a Martian who, like a bat, is wired much differently from how we are, let's look at what these ramifications might mean for vampire-human relations.

Vampires were once human, and perhaps they can remember what it was like to be human, yet humans have no such advantage with regard to vampires. We can fantasize about what it is like to be superhumanly strong and fast, to be able to fly, to have night vision, and to never see the sun. But there's more to being a vampire than merely being a human who possesses such characteristics. We struggle to comprehend the apparently eroticized and sublime vampire experience of the world, but finally we must admit that we may not have any idea of what it is like to be a vampire. Is their blood hunger, for example, essentially just like our hunger for food, only *really* intense? There seems to be some vague correlation. On the other hand, it also seems that vampire hunger, which is clearly eroticized and even produces a supernatural bond when a vampire feeds on a human, is not merely different from human hunger in degree but actually in kind. In the end it may be beyond our comprehension, like the subjective experience of a bat. Indeed, like other vampire stories, *True Blood* assures us that vampire experience is beyond human imagination (although perhaps doing the forbidden V gives us an inkling). Could that be why Sookie can't read their minds? Maybe vampires' imperviousness to human telepaths suggests that vampire otherness is much greater than their humanoid forms would suggest.

The upshot is that, despite the AVL's assurances, we simply cannot have the same ethical relationships with vampires as we do with other humans. Someone could argue that this concern is exaggerated since, first, we don't *really* know what our fellow humans experience either and, second, vampires do, after all, speak and act in what appear to be rational and intelligible ways. Still, the sorts of supernatural yearnings that vampires might be subject to, not to mention the way vampire maker–child and vampire-human blood-bond relationships seem to compromise if not destroy free will, are unlike anything seen in human society. Moreover, the ability of vampires to glamour humans—robbing them of free will, moral responsibility, and even their memories—could itself be an ethical deal breaker. How could humans ever be sure that vampires weren't abusing their power? As Aristotle famously asserts, one who is unable to live in the human polis is either a beast or a god. Vampires may be closer to the latter two categories than they are to us.[14]

Don't Sign Me Up for the Fellowship of the Sun—Just Yet!

Vampire mainstreaming is a serious challenge for a liberal human political society. Vampires are enmeshed in an illiberal, feudal political system that can't be reconciled with a liberal political order. Moreover, it's unclear whether vampires are capable of being good, rights-respecting, law-abiding citizens. So is mainstreaming a political and ethical nonstarter? Not necessarily. But the AVL needs to do much more to demonstrate that the vampire community is committed to mainstreaming. The process must start with dropping all of the secrecy and exposing vampire institutions and culture to the sunlight, as it were. That might destroy or drastically change these institutions and culture, but it must happen, insofar as they are based on the traditional murderous role that vampires have had in human society. It's just like an immigrant who moves from a country where it's acceptable to beat your wife to a liberal society: his practice and conception of marriage must be left behind. The AVL must proactively cooperate with human authorities to socialize or even "reeducate" vampires to enable them to integrate, and also to police vampires effectively and bring them under the rule of law. (There are some vampire cops in the Southern Vampire Mysteries, although they are not respected in the vampire community.) The AVL must win the vampire culture war and ensure that most vampires are genuinely committed to mainstreaming. These steps would at least be a reasonable start to a plausible vampire mainstreaming process.

But until that happens, we'd all better watch our necks!

NOTES

1. John Rawls, *Political Liberalism* (New York: Columbia Univ. Press, 1996), p. xx.

2. *Wisconsin v. Yoder*, 406 U.S. 205 (1972).

3. For more on these similarities, see Patricia Brace and Robert Arp's chapter in this volume, "Coming Out of the Coffin and Coming Out of the Closet."

4. See "True Blood Guide, Season 1: 'Escape From Dragon House' with Commentary from Alan Ball," true-blood.net/2009/10/28/true-blood-guide-season-1-escape-from-dragon-house-with-commentary-from-alan-ball/#tvg. Check out the opening credits scenes from the movie *Milk* for some black and white footage of raids on gay bars.

5. Episode 105, "Sparks Fly Out."

6. Vampire population is also a crucial issue for the consequences of mainstreaming, which *True Blood* hasn't mentioned. Harris's *All Together Dead* (New York: Ace Books, 2007) indicates that Louisiana was home to approximately forty vampires before

Hurricane Katrina hit (p. 10). We know that Louisiana is a very populous vampire kingdom, but we can only speculate as to the vampire populations of other states.

7. Episode 110, "I Don't Wanna Know." The source of this apparently universal body of law is not disclosed, so we do not know whether it is a magister-made, vampire common law, perhaps assembled into a compendium by a vampire William Blackstone (1723–1780), or a legal code jointly decreed by the several monarchs.

8. Episode 209, "I Will Rise Up."

9. Stephen Macedo, *Liberal Virtues: Citizenship, Virtue, and Community in Liberal Constitutionalism* (Oxford: Clarendon Press, 1990), pp. 271–272.

10. Chandran Kukathas, *The Liberal Archipelago: A Theory of Diversity and Freedom* (Oxford: Oxford Univ. Press, 2003), pp. 93–118.

11. Episode 110, "I Don't Wanna Know."

12. Thomas Nagel, "What Is It Like to Be a Bat?" *Philosophical Review* 83 (1974): 435–450.

13. For more on Nagel and his relevance to *True Blood*, see Fred Curry's chapter in this volume, "Keeping Secrets from Sookie."

14. *The Politics of Aristotle*, trans. Ernest Barker (Oxford: Oxford Univ. Press, 1958), p. 6.

UN-TRUE BLOOD

The Politics of Artificiality

Bruce A. McClelland

Since the eighteenth century vampires have served as a metaphor for a number of political, social, and psychological conflicts and complexes.[1] But now, in the first decade of the twenty-first century, we may be seeing a deeper and more nuanced transformation in the meaning of this apparently unkill-able idea. Anne Rice's *Interview with the Vampire* changed our relationship to the vampire by making him a mildly sympathetic first-person protagonist.[2] Now, thirty-five years later, in what is turning out to be a watershed period for the popular culture of vampires, this once horrific creature has finally lost the connection with absolute evil that has been an attribute of the vampire at least since the first American film version of *Dracula* in 1931.[3]

Past and Present

In the world of *True Blood* and the Southern Vampire Mysteries, the moral distance between human and vampire has been reduced to something akin to the political opposition that now polarizes contemporary America. Indeed, there are frequent visual references throughout the show to the talking-head antagonism that characterizes contemporary political discourse. Television talk shows discussing vampire rights provide on-screen commentaries on some plot point of the episode, while references to the growing cultural polarization between American Christian fundamentalism and progressive liberalism are frequent. For example, in a scene in Merlotte's Bar and Grill from an early episode of *True Blood*, there is a fleeting glimpse of an improbable poster, originally on the cover of the *Village Voice*, showing President George W. Bush about to bite the neck of the Statue of Liberty.[4]

In *True Blood*, the image of the vampire draws upon the classic attributes found in most vampire literature and films since *Dracula*, since these features are fundamental to the very identity of the vampire. Indeed, in American and European vampire narrative, the vampire's essence always seems to be defined by a minimal set of attributes that cannot be eliminated, even though they may be transformed. Thus the idea of the vampire as dead and the notion that vampires obtain sustenance from human life (blood or its analogues in psychic energy, health, corpulence, and so on) are *mandatory* aspects of the *True Blood* vampires, essential attributes without which vampires wouldn't be vampires.

While neither of these features by itself is necessary or sufficient to define the vampire over all periods and cultures, in contemporary popular culture there is no sense talking about vampires if these two conditions aren't present. So, unlike many recent self-conscious and often superficial transformations of the basic vampire story line, the *True Blood* vampires on the simplest level pose no real challenge to fundamental elements of the vampire myth. In fact some of the other more recent (post-*Dracula*) attributes of vampires—such as fangs, hypnotic power or "glamouring," superhuman strength, and the inability to tolerate sunlight and silver—are left alone as well. Some things are missing from the inventory of classical vampire traits, though, such as fear of Christian religious symbols (crucifixes, holy water) and shapeshifting. Nonvampires Sam Merlotte and Daphne Landry do the shapeshifting, while werewolves as a distinct class are present in the third season.[5]

A New Twist on an Old Narrative

True Blood does not redefine the vampire's habits or needs, but instead refocuses the vampire *community* and the politics of its interaction with the human community. The human community is largely represented by the residents of a small Louisiana bayou town facetiously named Bon Temps (French for "good times," a term commonly associated with Mardi Gras). The broader world beyond the bayou is seen in background television broadcasts and later in the second season's shift in backdrop to an amusingly named vampire-friendly hotel in Dallas, the Hotel Carmilla.[6]

The notion that vampires form communities is neither new nor surprising. To solve the problem of communities being able to thrive outside the mechanism of procreation, the contagious aspect (for example, the idea that you can become a vampire by, among other things, sharing blood with a vampire) that was attributed to the vampire only in the eighteenth century gradually became the means by which new vampires were created, allowing the population of the underground community of the undead to expand. A kind of miscegenation occurs as the result of the penetration of human flesh by a vampire's fangs, symbolizing genital contact.[7] There is an unmistakable eroticism in the contact between vampires and human beings that's responsible for the survival of the vampire race. It inevitably takes the form of a compulsion or need on the part of the vampire, so that the impulses of procreation and nutrition, sex and eating, are effectively merged in much contemporary vampire narrative.

Both the Southern Vampire Mysteries and *True Blood* take as a given this notion of a long-standing, near-immortal race of underground violent beings who require human blood to survive. But they put a new twist on the usual vampire narrative by investigating what would happen if the reason behind vampire violence—their *need* for human (and only human) blood—were eliminated. *True Blood* thus raises the question of what would happen to relations between human beings and vampires if a vampire's need for blood could be met by other means.

Coming Out of the Coffin

In *True Blood* and the Southern Vampire Mysteries, a new technology for synthesizing blood offers vampires the opportunity to "come out of the coffin." Many believe that with the right set of controls, vampires can reduce their level of marginalization from the human community. In the world of *True Blood*, this "reacquaintance" of the two cultures—the turned vampire with the unturned human—is tentative and not completely worked out. The longer threads of the first two seasons wrap around the complexities of adapting to this new situation and politically accommodating newly "out" vampires.

The vampires of *True Blood* are fictionalized stand-ins for actual oppressed or marginalized subcultures in the United States. While most of the obvious gags on the show refer to analogous travails of the gay community, any group seeking greater assimilation into the mainstream might also be represented by the vampires.[8] Importantly, the Western image of the vampire seems to be reverting from the purely evil to something more ambiguous. In Balkan folklore, where the vampire legend begins, the vampire served as a scapegoat, a creature whom the community could blame for whatever misfortunes it suffered, much like the witch in Western European countries.[9] The main difference is that while witches were living when they were tortured or immolated, vampires were corpses and therefore didn't feel a thing.[10] In any case, vampire folklore arose out of the community's need for someone—or some *thing*—to blame. But the possibility of recognizing the vampire as a victim has been effectively obscured since at least the mid-nineteenth century, when the philosopher Karl Marx (1818–1883) used the symbol of the purely demonic vampire to characterize the economic rape of the proletariat by the capitalist elites. Now, perhaps in part because of research that corrects some of the inaccurate histories of the vampire, a more complex and nuanced vampire can appear in fiction and even become a protagonist, as Bill Compton does in *True Blood*.[11]

True Blood may demonstrate a tolerance for vampire status that's meant to remind us of the manufactured and half-hearted increase in tolerance for various marginalized groups in the United States. But in the show, as in real life, there's an iron fist of an agenda hidden in the velvet glove. The commercial availability of a nutritional and palliative substance, TruBlood (TrueBlood in the novels), which quells the animalistic hunger for human blood sufficiently to allow vampires to enter human social situations without issue, is at base also a means of obtaining social control through technology. Although vampires are in the first stages of demanding and being granted certain rights, there are still residual animosities both between human beings and vampires, and among contentious factions within each of these groups. Within the vampire community, the fierce resistance to assimilation on the part of Eric Northman and the magister is a striking contrast to the final acquiescence to mortality—and hence humanness—exhibited by Godric (Godfrey in the novels). Their resistance may in fact be driven by concerns that the logical consequence of cultural assimilation could be the gradual disappearance of those cultural features that provide the vampire community (or any community, for that matter) with a sense of identity and cohesiveness. Although accomplished without violence, the end result is tantamount to genocide, which has the same goal of eliminating an entire community.

The Blood Is the Life

The communal substance that reveals the true nature of both human beings and vampires is the one that exposes their baser desires, namely blood, which comes in three flavors: human (with its various blood groups), vampire (V), and synthetic (TruBlood).[12] If, as we're told in both Deuteronomy 12:23 and *Dracula*, "the blood is the life," life itself has different existential features depending on blood type, and each type has symbolic importance for the relationship between human beings and vampires in *True Blood*.

Human blood symbolizes all that vampires lack in their empty narcissism. The actual behavior of human beings aside, inasmuch as the series shows it over and over again to be for the most part morally indistinguishable from vampire behavior, human blood is the common bond that is supposed to elevate living human beings above the dead. (Of course, no thought is given in the series to how this hierarchy implicitly privileges living human beings over every *other* form of life.)[13] Despite *True Blood*'s feigned irreligiosity, this notion of the supremacy of human blood as the essence of the human community is also an early Christian idea, implicit in Holy Communion.

At the other end of the spectrum is actual vampire blood, known colloquially as V-juice or just V. V has been designated an illicit substance, a drug that is verboten even in the relative Big Easiness of Bon Temps, because of its extreme and unpredictable effects on human physiology and psychology. A significant subplot of the first season of *True Blood* is built around the consequences of addiction to a substance so powerful that it has produced a class of criminal "vampire drainers" who deal in the stuff—and that takes the notion of aphrodisiac well beyond the four-hour priapisms promised by Cialis and Viagra. Jason Stackhouse, himself addicted to casual sex, is lured by Amy Burley into overdosing on V. We see the effects of ingesting this substance in scenes that are intentionally reminiscent of sixties ideas about the mind-altering benefits—and the horrific side effects of bad trips and flashbacks—of LSD and similar drugs.

Between these two extremes—the blood of human beings, with their naiveté, clumsiness, stupidity, and love, and the blood of vampires, with their heightened senses, wisdom, and vicious coldness—lies a third hemoderivative variant, TruBlood. TruBlood is an offering—a bribe, actually—by the human community to the vampires. It effectively asserts that (some of) the benefits of the human community can be granted to the inhuman as long as the latter accept and consume an inauthentic blood substitute and stop destroying human life to get the real thing. (It is not really explained why anyone with V running through their vessels would need or want human corpuscles, but such are the lapses of today's vampire narratives. Alan Ball has even acknowledged that he "embraces . . . the series' sloppiness" at tying up mythological and narrative details.)[14]

TruBlood is indeed a poor substitute for human blood. Like grape juice instead of wine at Holy Communion, it misses the point. Neither human beings nor vampires like the stuff. Human beings find it nauseating, and vampires (other than Bill, who, like many southerners, is nostalgic for pre–Civil War society and thus willing to acquire the taste) seem to think of it as a kind of why-bother near-beer. Given that neither human beings nor vampires care for it, what function does it serve in the narrative of *True Blood*?

Vampires as Ideal Consumers

Let's look more closely at what bottled TruBlood signifies in the drama surrounding the unlikely integration of these two groups, human and vampire, with a deep and perennial mistrust of each other. The existence of this substance—which not unintentionally rhymes with "true love"—is a sign that human medical technology is pursuing the goal of extending human life *almost* into the world of the dead. The quasi-immortality of vampires, attractive to human narcissists with few values beyond seeking eternal pleasure and stimulation, is dreadful to an older and presumably wiser vampire like Godric, who is tired of the damnation of playing out the same power struggles century after century. Even the vampire queen Sophie-Anne, who's only as old as the Industrial Revolution, reveals that despite her royal status, she suffers the unavoidable boredom of living a life with no foreseeable end. The unquestioned arrogance of the drive to extend life indefinitely, which produced the biomedical technology responsible for TruBlood, is able simultaneously to extend the "life" of the dead back into the world of the living, reducing the distance between the living and the dead (the vampires in *True Blood* always being referred to as dead rather than undead).[15]

So what might be the purpose of effectively bringing the dead back to life or allowing the nocturnally mobile community of ambulatory dead to engage politically with human beings? The primary motive is, of course, to diminish the vampires' hostility toward and power over the human community. Vampires are more powerful than human beings and therefore pose a threat. Even apart from their need for human blood, there seems to be something vaguely menacing about the typical conduct of vampires. Vampire society, persisting since ancient times, is organized hierarchically, along feudal lines of authority that stand in stark contrast to the undisciplined near-anarchy of legal and civil order in Bon Temps. Even the retributive violence that vampires carry out seems to follow a mafia-esque code of behavior.

It's no accident that *True Blood* and the Southern Vampire Mysteries are popular at a time when the American strategy of a global war on terror has begun to come under serious reconsideration. The implicit power of the vampires' alternative, dark society is analogous to the imagined, if not exactly imaginary, power ascribed to so-called terrorists, who work insidiously by infiltrating, converting, or destroying the innocent. The strategy for meeting this threat in the post-Bush world of *True Blood* ceases to be a fundamentalist crusade of the sort envisioned by the Fellowship of the Sun. Instead, the strategy is to curry favor with these ancient enemies, de-fang them, and bring them into the system. This approach seems to be a reasonable alternative to aggression, but it nevertheless also aims ultimately at eliminating the enemy. Synthetic blood is a trap. It draws the vampire out from his place of opposition, shifting a natural need away from its original object and toward dependency on the illusory benefit of consumption-based communion with human beings. As in the process of globalization, the need for the vampire to enter human society is based on the need to expand the marketplace to reach the ideal consumer, namely, one who's eternal. The strategy for pacifying the vampire community is to promote the benefit of assimilation by asserting the inherent superiority of the mainstream human world and the attractiveness of interaction with the living.

The Politics of Artificiality

Vampires hold a fascination for many residents of Bon Temps. For some, this fascination is due to the appeal of a society in which the will to violence, including sexual violence, does not need to be restrained, because there's no effective form of punishment. The freedom of the vampire, like the freedom of all dead monsters, derives from the absence of negative incentive with which to coerce them. Other residents of Bon Temps, including Sookie Stackhouse herself, can find no joy or acceptance with members of their own community and seem to be affected by a sympathetic deadness.

Deadening susceptibility to the trap of technological production naturally affects the high-tech commercial urban-media world of Dallas, where vampires have already been totally absorbed into a kind of glitzy hell. But it also creeps into the rural town of Bon Temps, especially in the second season of *True Blood*, when the residents fall under the spell of the maenad Maryann Forresters's alluring Dionysian hedonism, a disease brought into town when Maryann dangles the illusion of opulence and wealth before the miserable and impoverished Tara Thornton. Tara and other local residents abandon their ordinary lives and, presumably, their principles when they are mesmerized into participating in an extended orgy that is actually a preparation for human sacrifice. Maryann's disingenuous promise of personal transformation is so alluring that no one bothers to consider the possibility that she doesn't have their true interests at heart.

One lesson we might draw from the Maryann story is that the human community can easily be bought off, tossing aside its principles in exchange for the promise of a glamorous existence filled with unbridled pleasure. It's precisely because of its moral weakness that the human community reveals its insecurity in the face of the more disciplined vampire society. Aware of its own susceptibility to self-absorbed abandonment and consumption, human society regards the vampire community as hostile, since its essential nature and organization, not to mention power and capacity for violence, threaten to expose the human community's moral lassitude.[16] We have to wonder whether the attempt to bring the vampires into the human world by encouraging them to consume TruBlood represents a drive to ensnare them in the same dependencies and lack of freedom that characterize our society, one that many would characterize as lacking belief, trust, or a deep link to nature.

In the world of *True Blood*, human beings are time and again shown to be the inferior race, despite their capacity for warm devotion and family bonding. The rescue of human beings from vampires or other supernatural forces, such as Maryann's pseudo-Dionysian minions, is always orchestrated by inhuman or more-than-human beings: Bill, Eric, Sam, or Sookie. The special powers wielded by these supernatural individuals, at least some of whom are unaccountably sympathetic toward ordinary human beings, are both appealing and threatening to the residents of Bon Temps. At the same time that human beings covet these extra-human characteristics, they display a self-righteous refusal or inability to participate in the world of the dangerous supernatural by engaging the vampire community on its own terms. They have given up the possibility—and the risk—of such participation in exchange for "the comforts of life."

TruBlood, the synthetic substance that, at least metaphorically, brings vampires down to the dulled sensory level of human beings as much as V brings human senses toward the primal and feral, provides an artificial communion that brings vampires closer, so that we can look at them unafraid. But in doing that, it only reaffirms our own self-satisfaction with the politics of artificiality.

NOTES

1. See Nina Auerbach, *Our Vampires, Ourselves* (Chicago: Univ. of Chicago Press, 1997).

2. Anne Rice, *Interview with the Vampire* (New York: Ballantine Books, 1997).

3. People in the United States became acquainted with the vampire mostly through the movies rather than through Bram Stoker's 1897 novel, and hundreds of vampire movies have been made in the United States since 1931, when the Universal Studios version of *Dracula* was first released. In the novel, there is no incontrovertible evidence that Count Dracula is either dead or supernatural, since all of the evidence against him is circumstantial (the structure of the novel is epistolary). Films, however, with their linear structure, have caused us to lose any sense of ambiguity about the nature of the vampire, and it took several decades before the vampire could be seen as a strongly sympathetic (alienated) or at least not totally evil being. For a more detailed discussion of this point, see chapter 9 of my book *Slayers and Their Vampires*, "From Vienna to London" (Ann Arbor: Univ. of Michigan Press, 2006).

4. Episode 104, "Escape from the Dragon House." You can also see this image of Bush at www.observer.com/2008/media/2004-village-voice-cover-makes-cameo-hbo-vampire-series.

5. Public statement by Alan Ball, Virginia Film Festival, Culbreth Theater, University of Virginia, Charlottesville, VA, November 7, 2009.

6. These episodes were in fact filmed at the Sofitel in Los Angeles. *Carmilla* is the name of a famous vampire novella published in 1872 by the Irish writer Sheridan LeFanu.

7. In Bram Stoker's *Dracula*, for example, it is never clear whether Lucy becomes a vampire because Dracula has drunk her blood, or because he has made her drink his.

8. See Robert Arp and Patricia Brace's chapter in this volume, "Coming Out of the Coffin and Coming Out of the Closet."

9. For more on scapegoating, see Kevin J. Corn and George A. Dunn's chapter in this volume, "Let the Bon Temps Roll: Sacrifice, Scapegoats, and Good Times."

10. The scapegoat aspect of the vampire is discussed at length in my doctoral dissertation, "Sacrifice, Scapegoat, Vampire: The Social and Religious Origins of the Bulgarian Folkloric Vampire" (Univ. of Virginia, 1999). There, and in subsequent writings, I demonstrate that the vampire is marked as a scapegoat by having special ritual features and physical characteristics.

11. See, for example, my book *Slayers and Their Vampires*, and Jan Perkowski, *Vampire Lore* (Bloomington, IN: Slavica, 2006).

12. It is interesting that the synthetic blood is supposedly developed by the Japanese. In Japanese culture, partially as a consequence of the publication in 1927 of a famous paper by Takeji Furukawa, there is a common belief that a person's blood group indicates his or her personality, temperament, and compatibility with others. (Furukawa's paper, "A Study of Temperament in Blood Types," was reprinted in the *Journal of Social Psychology*, 1 (1930): 494–509.) TruBlood is available in an assortment of blood groups, but nothing further is made of a supposed connection with the typology of personality or disposition.

13. For more on how human beings have privileged themselves above every other form of life, see Ariadne Blayde and George A. Dunn's chapter in this volume, "Pets, Cattle, and Higher Life Forms on *True Blood*."

14. Remarks at the Virginia Film Festival, Culbreth Theater, University of Virginia, Charlottesville, VA, November 8, 2009.

15. The notion of mechanically recreating or imitating life by technologically invigorating the dead is also present in *Frankenstein*, a movie about the creation of a monster by a scientist, Dr. Henry Frankenstein. The movie premiered in 1931, the same year as *Dracula*.

16. This sort of projection is present in various forms of imperialism, where the colonialists see the colonized as savage and primitive; yet it is often the colonialists who act in a more savage manner, committing genocide or various forms of barbarism. See Michael Taussig, *Mimesis and Alterity: A Particular History of the Senses* (New York: Routledge, 1993).

PART THREE

"THEIR VERY BLOOD IS SEDUCTIVE": EROS, SEXUALITY, AND GENDER

COMING OUT OF THE COFFIN AND COMING OUT OF THE CLOSET

Patricia Brace and Robert Arp

The world of Sookie Stackhouse is rife with analogies between homosexuals and vampires. Think, for example, of Charlaine Harris's description of vampires' entrance into mainstream society, referred to as the "Great Revelation," in *Living Dead in Dallas*: "When the Japanese had perfected the synthetic blood that actually enabled vampires to live without drinking human blood, it had been possible for vampires to come out of the coffin"—an obvious allusion to gays coming out of the closet.[1] Or consider the play on the Fred Phelpsian slogan "God hates fags" found in the lit-up sign in the opening credits of *True Blood* that displays the message "God hates fangs." In fact, the premier episode of *True Blood* mocks the idea that one can spot a vampire just from his mannerisms and the clothes he wears when it turns out that the vampire in the all-night market is *not* the Goth clerk harassing two teenagers, but the potbellied, flannel-wearing "Billy Bob" who pops fang and terrorizes the clerk as a wannabe.[2] Still, the outsider's style is often imitated.

Just as "metrosexual" queer-eyed men imitate the grooming habits of gays in our world, fang-bangers adopt a vampirelike pallor and wear black lipstick in bars like Fangtasia. And the end of season 2 makes a political gesture, as plane tickets to Vermont accompany a vampire marriage proposal in an obvious reference to Vermont as one of five states that currently allow same-sex unions.[3]

In her books Harris introduces several characters who are homosexual, some of whom are supernatural as well. In addition to Merlotte's human African American short-order cook Lafayette Reynolds, there is the arrogant fairy Claude (a walking double-entendre, since he is both gay and a magical fairy with supernatural powers). *True Blood* makes Lafayette more prominent by increasing his screen time, his importance to the plotline, and the complexity of his character, and by choosing not to kill him off at the end of the season. Lafayette is, of course, connected to the supernatural world through the gay vampire Eddie Gauthier, who in return for sexual favors supplies Lafayette with blood to be sold as the powerful drug known as V.[4]

Eddie is an interesting creation, because he blurs the line between coming out of the coffin and coming out of the closet. Eddie was closeted most of his life, even marrying and having a son. When he was forced to face his sexuality, he left his family and decided to go to a gay bar for the first time. Middle-aged, overweight, and balding, he was undesirable and humiliated. But then he noticed that a vampire, no more attractive than himself, was mobbed by young men eager for his attentions. For Eddie the choice was clear: he leaped from closet to coffin.

In this chapter, we're going to explore the parallels between vampirism and homosexuality. Should either vampirism or homosexuality be considered unnatural? How about immoral? And is there any reason to think either vampires or homosexuals might not be deserving of the same rights and privileges as any other human being or, for vampires, any *living* human being?

"Vampires Are an Unnatural Abomination"

In the sixth book of the Southern Vampire Mysteries, *Definitely Dead*, the local Catholic and Episcopal priests come into Merlotte's for dinner one evening. This prompts some exposition from the narrator, waitress Sookie Stackhouse, on their respective Churches' positions on vampires:

> The Catholic Church was at that moment holding convocation to decide whether the church would declare all vampires damned and an anathema to Catholics, or to accept them into the fold as potential converts. The Episcopal Church had voted against accepting vampires as priests, though they were allowed to take communion—but a substantial slice of the laity said that would be over their dead bodies. Unfortunately, most of them didn't comprehend how possible that was.[5]

The Catholic priest chides Sookie for speaking to the local vampire Bill Compton, referring to him as "the imp of hell," and both priests let her know they consider vampires to be unsuitable company. The Episcopal Church is no stranger to controversy over the issues surrounding homosexuality. The ordination of gay men and women, the vote to allow priests to officiate at same-sex marriage ceremonies, and the 2003 consecration of Gene Robinson as the first openly gay bishop have all caused a potential schism in the modern Episcopal Church.

In Sookie's world, as we would expect, Islam doesn't treat vampires well either. In the third book of the series, *Club Dead*, Sookie describes the fallout from the Great Revelation: "The vampires in the predominantly Islamic nations had fared the worst. You don't even want to know what happened to the undead spokesman in Syria, though perhaps the female vamp in Afghanistan died an even more horrible—and final—death."[6] Under Sharia law, the undead would possibly receive the same punishment as homosexuals—the death penalty in some countries—because their very existence might be seen as unnatural and anathema.

It seems as if every major religion (and a lot of the minor ones too) has some written or oral ban on "one man lying with another man" that's punishable by losing a penis, a testicle, your life, or all three. The universality of this ban is unsurprising, since religious laws are a reflection of human desires and anxieties, and the patriarchal cultures that wrote these religious laws feared any kind of uncontrolled sexuality. But wouldn't God have created all variations of sexuality for *some* decent reason?[7]

In Matthew 23:27–28, Jesus Christ is reported to have said:

> Woe to you, teachers of the law and Pharisees, you hypocrites! You are like whitewashed tombs which look beautiful on the outside but on the inside are full of dead men's bones and everything unclean. In the same way, on the outside you appear to people as righteous but on the inside you are full of hypocrisy and wickedness.

In *True Blood*, the members of the ultra-right-wing Fellowship of the Sun are like the Pharisees, "beautiful on the outside"—perhaps even by design, since they specifically recruit the photogenic blond "himbo" Jason Stackhouse as a sort of poster boy. But the main thrust of their preaching isn't beautiful at all, for they preach that all "vampires are an unnatural abomination" and that the Fellowship is doing "God's work" in attempting to rid the world of them.[8] For all their righteous appearance, the Fellowship's hypocrisy shows when they use terrorism to attack vampires and any humans associated with them. On Steve Newlin's orders, a true believer straps on a suicide bomber's vest, wraps himself in silver chains and spikes, and detonates himself in the Dallas vampire nest, an act referred to in *Living Dead in Dallas* as "the Dallas Midnight Massacre" and "touted in all the newsmagazines as the perfect example of a hate crime."[9] The Fellowship of the Sun reemerges in *All Together Dead*, where there is an Oklahoma City–style bombing attack on a national vampire summit. And in *Dead Until Dark*, a vigilante mob, not directly associated with the Fellowship, but sharing much of their worldview, torches a Louisiana nest during the day while the four vampires within are asleep.

We're Here, We're Vampire . . . Get Used to It!

Those who hate gays and vampires are quick to point out that their lifestyles are not natural. But what is natural? To address the question of naturalness, we need to distinguish between *orientation* and *action*. Let's say that *orientation* refers to the basic, primal, instinctive desires and wants that make someone a homosexual or a heterosexual. On the other hand, *action* refers to what it sounds like, the actions and other behaviors that stem from an orientation. Some people think that your sexual orientation is something that you choose, that you choose to be gay or straight.[10] However, most studies of homosexuals reveal that their orientation has been present since early childhood, long before they have enough life experience to make a fully conscious, rational choice of orientation.[11] Further, there have been some brain and genetic studies to support the theory that homosexuals are gay by nature, the "gayture" hypothesis.[12] Despite these findings, there are still "deprogrammers" and "reparative therapy" groups run by church organizations that believe they can "cure" people of gayness.[13] But there's no reason to believe that anyone would choose his or her sexual orientation. Scientific data aside, would you *choose* to be the outcast of every society? Would you want to have to *choose* between being locked in the closet or coming out of the closet and running the risk of being ridiculed or even killed?

A similar choice is faced by the vampires in Harris's books. They are not able to return to being human any more than a homosexual can be reprogrammed to be straight. A vampire's "orientation," so to speak, is vampire. So where does the question of nature or nurture come in for a vampiric "orientation?" Vampires seem to be unlike gays in that we can't say that vampires are born that way. After all, vampires are made, not born. But there is a still a parallel to being born either gay or straight, for once you become a vampire, there's no returning to a human existence. To become a vampire is to be "reborn" into a new existence—and for some, like Eddie, it is a very deliberate choice, made for the benefits he perceives he will derive from being a vampire. Others are made vampires against their will; their only choice was to die or be reborn vampire.

In *True Blood* we see vampires being made on three different occasions. A flashback sequence shows Civil War soldier Bill Compton accepting food and shelter from the seemingly genteel southern widow Lorena, who attacks and turns him into a vampire without his consent. Viking-era vampire Eric Northman is near death, lying on his funeral bier, when the one-thousand-year-old boy vampire, Godric, turns him.[14] And the innocent Christian virgin, Jessica Hamby, is made a vampire by Bill, who is being punished for killing another vampire.

In some cases, giving up mortality and becoming vampire is viewed by the victim as a positive change. Pam, who manages Eric's bar, Fangtasia, revels in her existence as a vampire, despite the fact that Eric made her against her will. Jessica greatly prefers the freedom from her father's beatings and the opportunity to date that her new existence gives her, but rails against the limits her new "daddy" places on her. One's first loyalty is always to one's maker, and as with human parents and children, most vampires take the responsibility of being a maker and the bond it creates very seriously. For example, much of season 2 of *True Blood* centers around just these sorts of bonds: Eric's efforts to free Godric, his beloved maker, whom he believes has been captured by the Fellowship of the Sun, is contrasted with the twisted bond Bill shares with his maker, Lorena, which is very different in turn from the paternal bond he is trying to establish with his willful creation, Jessica. Like the parent-child bond among human beings, the bond between a vampire and his or her maker can be healthy or dysfunctional, not to mention all the shades in between. The relationship and its attendant obligations closely parallel the "natural" filial relationships around which human reproduction is structured. In short, if we think of being a vampire as an "orientation," by analogy to a human sexual orientation, then it appears to be equally natural.

Depending on who's counting, only five to fifteen percent of the world's population is homosexual in orientation.[15] Likewise, humans still far outnumber vampires in the *True Blood* universe. For centuries vampires either lived totally apart from human society or attempted to "pass" as human, like gays trying to pass as straight. When the vampire ruling hierarchy decided to make the Great Revelation, some vampires, like Bill Compton, attempted to mainstream into human society, living primarily on synthetic blood and taking up a new kind of relationship with human beings. The old way of interacting with humanity was as predator to prey, which parallels some of the worst fears of homophobia—that a homosexual predator will attack or coerce an unwilling person into homosexual acts. In the new world of open relations between human beings and vampires, the former can usually choose how they interact with the latter—some sell their blood as a form of legal prostitution, allowing vampires to feed on them for profit, while others, such as Sookie and Jessica's beau, Hoyt Fortenberry, have romantic relationships with vampires and share blood as part of lovemaking. These relationships resemble ordinary nonpredatory sexual relationships between human beings.

If normal means being average or in the majority, then normalcy is something that will always elude both vampires and gays. But being normal can also be defined as acceptance into mainstream society. Normalizing the presence of any formerly excluded subgroup is usually an incremental process. There are certain businesses—travel agencies, bookstores, clothing stores, media outlets, film companies—that cater specifically to the gay market, but homosexuality begins to become truly normalized only when, for example, a gay character appears in mainstream media that reach *both* heterosexual and homosexual audiences. One of the best-known examples of this was when Ellen DeGeneres came out in her personal life and on her sitcom *Ellen* in 1997. What caused a media frenzy in 1997 seems normal today; since 2003 she has hosted her eponymous multiple Emmy Award–winning talk show and is a beloved national icon.

In Harris's books, the vampire hierarchy uses the media as a tool to establish the normalcy of the vampire subculture. There are vampire radio stations (one of which is KDED), talk shows, Web sites, and magazines like *Fang*, which Sookie describes as the vampire version of *People*. She also tells us that the first network television portrayal of a vampire is on a teen soap opera, which parallels the appearance of the gay character Jodie Dallas on the 1970s television show *Soap* and the gay teenager Jack McPhee on the 1990s teen soap *Dawson's Creek*.

When we categorize someone as unnatural, we often imply that the person is mentally disordered or evil.[16] Bigoted negative stereotypes, such as "all homosexuals are pedophiles trolling playgrounds or the Internet for little boys" derive from this implication. Such stereotypes are usually put forward by hate groups. In *True Blood*, Fellowship of the Sun leader Steve Newlin describes vampires in a way reminiscent of antihomosexual hate speech, referring to "their endless role of seduction and temptation."[17] Hate groups rely on fear to perpetuate their message of intolerance. The Fellowship of the Sun trots out traditional vampire myths to recruit for their cult. The myths tell us that vampires are evil and soulless, can't be seen in mirrors, are repelled by crosses, garlic, and holy water, are powerless on holy ground, and must always kill the humans from which they derive blood. The truth is that before the invention of synthetic blood, vampires did typically prey on human beings, but without necessarily having to kill them. Vampire Bill disproves some of those other stereotypes when he comes to Adele Stackhouse's church to speak at a meeting of the Descendants of the Glorious Dead.

Sex and Feeding, Penis and Fangs

It should go without saying that your sexuality is no indication of where you will lie on the broad human spectrum of personality, intelligence, and temperament. The same is true of the vampires in *True Blood*. A vampire can be a vainglorious jerk, or a vampire can be kind, generous, and gifted (and sometimes all of these at the same time, Mr. Northman!). Likewise, your sexual orientation doesn't limit the contributions you can make to society. Throughout history many people of artistic genius were homosexual. We could begin by mentioning Socrates, Michelangelo, Oscar Wilde, Alan Turing, Ludwig Wittgenstein, and Elton John, but a more complete list would fill a book.[18] The stigma of stereotyping and the fear of losing the respect of their fans and peers have kept many talented homosexuals closeted, worried that they will be seen only as their sexual orientation, negating every other part of them in the public eye.

The opposite, however, seems to be true for the vampires we meet in *True Blood* and the Southern Vampire Mysteries. They want to be identified primarily as vampires, which means they choose to be defined by a single action that ensures their survival—drinking human blood, synthetic or real. They run the gamut of age, national origin, race, and sexual orientation, but none of that matters—a vampire's race, creed, and color is *vampire*. Bill's refrain "I am Vampire," not "I am *a* vampire," makes this clear. He announces "I am Vampire" in the same way someone else might say "I'm gay" or "black" or "Presbyterian." It's an identity, as a lawyer who argued a housing discrimination case for a vampire, explains in *Living Dead in Dallas*: "But you know what, Sookie? Vampires aren't American. They aren't even black or Asian or Indian. They aren't Rotarians or Baptists. They're all plain vampires. That's their color and their religion and their nationality."[19]

Let's compare the physical aspects of a homosexual relationship to the vampire's actions of feeding on a human being. Both are often mysterious and therefore threatening to people who have not participated in them, creating a certain "ick" factor. It seems to us, however, that it is possible for a gay man or woman to be in an intimate, consensual, and healthy sexual relationship in which both parties are fully rational and take full responsibility for their actions, practice safe sex, and have the same moral obligations to each other that any two people engaged in a physical relationship have. If either party withheld consent or lacked the ability to consent (as happens in the case of forcible or statutory rape), that would make it an immoral relationship, regardless of the sexual orientation of the participants.

In *True Blood* there are many examples of healthy and unhealthy sexual relationships, both between humans and between humans and vampires. Sookie's childhood was plagued by visits from her pedophile "funny uncle" Bartlett, who molested her repeatedly. Despite this childhood abuse, she is able to have a positive loving relationship with Bill, expressed in both a sexual and vampiric way, the latter involving Bill's biting and feeding on her. The obvious physical parallels between sex and the way a vampire feeds are erection (of the penis or the fangs) and penetration (of one's partner's flesh). The vampire's fangs, as envisioned in the series, are retractable and appear only when he or she is sexually aroused, excited by blood, or angered. When Bill and Sookie kiss for the first time, she's frightened when his fangs pop out. When they finally consummate their relationship, he penetrates her simultaneously with both penis and fangs, heightening the pleasure for both of them. But because he has asked her permission before he does either action, we would consider this a healthy sexual interaction between vampire and human. What Lorena did in making Bill a vampire, however, was the equivalent of rape, an immoral act because she took away his right to choose. If he didn't take her blood, he would die—and how many of us could refuse, given only those options?

The sexual acts that Bill and his partners engage in cannot produce a child—vampires are infertile. Here the proponent of naturalness could step forward and argue (as many do against homosexuality) that "ideally, according to the *natural view of natural activities*, sex should be between a man and a woman and should be open to the possibility of procreation. After all, this is what such a natural activity should lead to." They may even say something further like this: "Any other kind of sexual interaction is unnatural and hence immoral." This line of thinking has obvious flaws, however. For starters, it makes most people who have sex immoral, since their aim is usually something other than procreation. Lots of heterosexual couples can't or don't want to procreate for one reason or another, yet they still engage in sexual intercourse and other nonprocreative sexual acts such as oral sex. Do we want to ban them from sex just because they can't or choose not to procreate? How dare they attempt to have sex for something like *love* or *intimacy*! This is the remnant of a twisted antisex, antibody, antipleasure way of thinking that still exists in almost all of the world's major religions and has made its way into current customs and laws.

Don't Eat Your Date, Jessica!

If you're gay and have the misfortune to live in all but a few locations in the world today, chances are you're not going to be able to get married, adopt children, have access to your partner's health insurance, be taken care of in your old age, and many other things that heterosexuals take for granted. That's another reason many gay people and *True Blood* vampires have chosen to stay in their respective closets or coffins. If coming out means you might suffer limitations on, or even the outright loss of, your societal rights and privileges, nondisclosure may seem like the best option. The fight over who has the right to marry, a primary concern of homosexuals in mainstream American society, finds an almost exact parallel in the debate over human-vampire unions in *True Blood*.

Child rearing is another hot-button issue. Despite the homophobic belief that children raised by gay parents will be somehow damaged—turning gay, doing drugs, becoming underachievers—there is no indication that children of gay parents are much different (neither more healthy nor more dysfunctional) from those raised in traditional families.[20] If we make the same arguments for vampire parents, however, we need to differentiate between human children and vampire "offspring." Because of their need for day sleep, vampires may not make the best parents for human children. But a subplot of *True Blood*'s second season follows Bill's struggle to manage his vampire teenage daughter, the willful Jessica. She pushes his guilt button by reminding him that it's his fault she's a vampire, and she tests boundaries on issues like using the car and dating privileges just like a human teenager. Unlike human fathers, Bill is saddled with the added problem of making sure she doesn't eat her date.

Deserving of Equal Rights under the Law

If one can identify a whole group or class of people as unnatural or less than human based on their inclinations and actions, then one might conclude that their lives don't have the same value as our lives. From the suffragettes to the civil rights movements of the 1960s, to the fight for the Equal Rights Amendment and the movement for gay rights—the underclass and the oppressed have always used the available public forums (such as television, radio, and print media), in addition to the legal system and the legislature to fight for their rights. The vampires on *True Blood* have a national agenda, including Washington lobbyists pushing the

Vampire Rights Amendment (VRA), clever commercials showing everyday Americans coming out as vampires, and spokesperson Nan Flanagan of the American Vampire League (AVL) appearing on *Real Time with Bill Maher* and debating the Fellowship of the Sun's original leader, the Reverend Theodore Newlin (Steve's father). Echoing the intolerance of hate groups like the Ku Klux Klan toward African Americans, Jews, and homosexuals, the reverend refuses even to dialogue with Nan.

In the wake of the Great Revelation, vampires have had to work hard for the limited civil rights they've gained. In the ninth book of the series, *Dead and Gone*, Harris reveals that even seven years later,

> they hadn't yet obtained full rights and privileges under the law. Legal marriage and inheritance of property were still forbidden in a few states, and vampires were barred from owning certain businesses. The human casino lobby had been successful in banning the vamps from direct ownership of gambling establishments . . . and though vampires could be police officers and firefighters, vampire doctors were not accepted in any field that included treating patients with open wounds. Vampires weren't allowed in competition sports, either.[21]

Again we see obvious parallels to the limits placed on groups such as homosexuals who have been deemed unworthy of the same rights and privileges as other Americans. Vampires have acquired some personal protection from harm, however. Staking a vampire is equivalent to murdering a human being, and deliberately victimizing someone because he or she is a vampire carries additional penalties accorded to hate crimes.

Vampires still face special dangers after coming out of the coffin. Bill is lured from Merlotte's on the night of his first visit by the Rattrays, a criminal couple who intend to drain his blood and kill him in the process. Held down by silver at his neck and wrists, arms outstretched, his blood draining into collection bags, Bill is in effect being objectified and crucified, made to shed his blood simply for the Rattrays' own profit and addictions. To them, Bill isn't human, so his death won't matter. Since blood is their objective, it is tempting to see them as merely turning the tables, making the vampire a victim of human bloodsuckers for a change. The difference is that until the invention of the Japanese synthetic, human blood was necessary for a vampire's survival. It was what they ate, and all they *could* eat to maintain their existence. Collecting, selling, and ingesting vampire blood, by contrast, are not necessary for human survival. They are in fact dangerous practices and, as we are repeatedly reminded, criminal acts punishable by law.

Still, there's always good legal money to be made catering to the subgroups market. Just as many bars, beverage companies, hotels, dating services, cruise lines, travel agencies, and clothing manufacturers cater to gay consumers, vampires and vampire wannabes (let's call them "fang-hangers" to differentiate them from those who have sex with vampires, the "fang-bangers") are also a target market. For example, the bonus features on the season 1 *True Blood* DVD include a clever advertisement for a human-vampire dating service, a direct reference to the recent eHarmony.com controversy. Before a lawsuit was settled in 2009, the online dating service eHarmony didn't accept gay clients. Another company, Chemistry.com, moved to fill that niche by using commercials with attractive singles who mused about what was wrong after their applications to a dating site had been rejected. The *True Blood* ads capture the look and tone of those ads so well you'd almost believe such a service exists.

As we've seen, then, coming out of the coffin or the closet these days requires courage. Let's hope, pray, and act so that in the future anyone, regardless of sexual orientation, religion, or race, whether living or dead, can find acceptance along with basic human and civil rights in Bon Temps and your hometown, too.

NOTES

1. Charlaine Harris, *Living Dead in Dallas* (New York: Ace Books, 2002), p. 26.

2. This seems to be a salute to the opening scene of the first episode of Joss Whedon's TV series *Buffy the Vampire Slayer*. An innocent-looking blond coed sneaks into the high school after dark with a dark-haired bad boy, but Whedon turns our expectations upside down when the *girl* morphs into a vampire and kills him.

3. As of this writing the other states are Connecticut, Iowa, Massachusetts, and New Hampshire. Washington, D. C also grants same-sex marriages. California briefly approved same-sex marriage before it was voted down under Proposition 8 in 2008. Maine's law was repealed by a ballot initiative in November 2009. Three states currently have pre-1996 laws or court rulings that specifically ban gay marriage: Maryland, Wisconsin, and Wyoming. For more state-by-state information see Sheri Stritof and Bob Stritof, "Same Sex Marriage License Laws: United States," marriage.about.com/cs/marriagelicenses/a/samesexcomp.htm.

4. In *True Blood*'s world, vampire blood, or V, is a valuable street drug, combining the effects of Viagra, crack, and LSD. In the real world, HIV/AIDs has been purported by some to be a punishment for engaging in homosexual acts. Bodily fluids are seen as poisonous and death dealing, and the use of "safe sex" practices such as condoms, dental dams, and so on is the price one has to pay for indulging in the risk of sex. In *True Blood* this is turned on its ear because rather than causing death, vampire blood brings ecstasy and life; for example, repairing Sookie's and Lafayette's serious physical injuries.

5. Charlaine Harris, *Definitely Dead* (New York: Ace Books, 2006), p. 12.

6. Charlaine Harris, *Club Dead* (New York: Ace Books, 2003), p. 5.

7. For more on this issue, see Jack Rogers, *Jesus, the Bible and Homosexuality: Explode the Myths, Heal the Church* (Louisville: Westminster John Knox Press, 2006), and Daniel Helminiak, *What the Bible Really Says about Homosexuality* (San Francisco: Alamo Square Distributors, 2000).

8. See Fellowship of the Sun Web site at www.fellowshipofthesun.org/reflections/index.html#damnation.

9. Harris, *Living Dead in Dallas*, p. 218.

10. See, for example, the wacky ideas in Joseph Nicolosi and Linda Nicolosi, *A Parent's Guide to Preventing Homosexuality* (Downers Grove, IL: InterVarsity Press, 2002).

11. Eric Marcus, *Is It a Choice? Answers to 300 of the Most Frequently Asked Questions about Gays and Lesbians* (San Francisco: Harper, 1993); Neil Risch, Elizabeth Squires-Wheeler, and Bronya Keats, "Male Sexual Orientation and Genetic Evidence," *Science* 262 (1993): 2063–2064.

12. Simon LeVay, "A Difference in Hypothalamic Structure between Heterosexual and Homosexual Men," *Science* 253 (1991): 1034–1037; Dean Hamer, Stella Hu, Victoria Magnuson, Nan Hu, and Angela Pattatucci, "A Linkage between DNA Markers on the X Chromosome and Male Sexual Orientation," *Science* 261 (1993): 321–327.

13. These include Exodus International, whose president, Alan Chambers, recently published a book titled *Leaving Homosexuality: A Practical Guide for Men and Women Looking for a Way Out* (Eugene, OR: Harvest House, 2009), in which he argues that a homosexual lifestyle and Christianity are mutually exclusive, so if one can overcome an

inborn same-sex sexual orientation and abstain from all such relationships, then one can be a Christian.

14. Eric is turned under different circumstances in the Southern Vampire Mysteries. In *Dead and Gone* (New York: Ace Books, 2009), we find out that while on his way home from courting a potential bride, Eric was attacked and turned by an ancient Roman vampire, Appius Livius Ocella. A sexual predator, the former Legionnaire also raped Eric, who could not refuse his maker. This is very different from his relationship to Godric, who refers to Eric as his "father, brother and son," but never as lover.

15. Preeti Pathela, Anjum Hajat, Julia Schillinger, Susan Blank, Randall Sell, and Farzad Mostashari, "Discordance between Sexual Behavior and Self-Reported Sexual Identity: A Population-Based Survey of New York City Men," *Annals of Internal Medicine* 145 (2006): 416–425.

16. For years psychologists considered homosexuality to be a disorder, but they have reconsidered this label. See Irving Bieber, "On Arriving at the American Psychiatric Association Decision on Homosexuality," NARTH Bulletin 7 (1999): 15–23.

17. See the Fellowship of the Sun Web site at www.fellowshipofthesun.org/reflections/index.html#damnation.

18. And in fact it does. See Thomas Cowan, *Gay Men and Women Who Enriched the World* (Boston: Alyson Publications, 1992); also, the articles in Martin Duberman, Martha Vicinus, and George Chauncey, eds., *Hidden from History: Reclaiming the Gay and Lesbian Past* (New York: Meridian, 1990).

19. Harris, *Living Dead in Dallas*, p. 144.

20. There are many of these studies, but for a representative one see N. Anderssen, C. Amlie, and E. Ytteroy, "Outcomes for Children with Lesbian or Gay Parents: A Review of Studies from 1978 to 2000," *Scandinavian Journal of Psychology* 43 (2002): 335–351.

21. Harris, *Dead and Gone*, p. 73.

"I AM SOOKIE, HEAR ME ROAR!"

Sookie Stackhouse and Feminist Ambivalence

Lillian E. Craton and Kathryn E. Jonell

In Charlaine Harris's *From Dead to Worse*, the eighth book in the Southern Vampire Mysteries, Sookie Stackhouse is tempted to give in to the sexual advances of her sometime boss, vampire Eric Northman. Proud of her resistance, she invokes the title of Helen Reddy's anthem and the most recognizable catchphrase of twentieth-century feminism: "I am woman, hear me roar." This reference reminds readers of both Sookie's feminist appeal—particularly her independence and her self-determination—and the way her story reflects a feminist perspective.

While there's no one single definition of feminism, contemporary feminists have increasingly directed their energies toward enhancing individual experience and cultural diversity, while at the same time promoting equality for everyone. Feminists of this generation have grown up feeling entitled to the rights and privileges won by previous generations, but not all women have yet achieved equal access to the fruits of those earlier struggles.

Sookie's story, as told in the Southern Vampire Mysteries and as depicted in the HBO series *True Blood*, is worth hearing not just because of its exciting supernatural adventures but because she's truly a woman of her times, living out all of the complexities and ambiguities of contemporary feminism while maintaining a tough, spunky "girl power" appeal.

Incendiary Identities

Sookie makes her way through the world as a working-class, "disabled" (or psychically gifted) woman, meeting members of other groups that are also struggling for equality and acceptance. An enlightened woman, Sookie wants to support their rights but finds that effort difficult when, for example, she discovers the violent and hierarchical attitudes imbedded within supernatural cultures.[1] Her commitment to diversity is challenged when both supernatural creatures and religious extremists attack her. Take, for instance, Sookie's discomfort with the Shreveport Were pack's inclusion of sexual intercourse as part of the initiation of a new pack leader in *Dead as a Doornail*, the fifth book of the Southern Vampire Mysteries. Her response is similar to the tension felt by many feminists who support the rights of others to determine their own culture while also worrying about groups that still expect women to wear a burka. Sookie's struggle mirrors that of Hugo, a minor character in season 2 of *True Blood* and *Living Dead in Dallas*, the second book of the Southern Vampire Mysteries. "I was convinced vampires had the same civil rights as other people," he reports, adding that since then he's concluded that "vampires aren't American. They aren't even black or Asian or Indian. They aren't Rotarians or Baptists. They're all just plain vampires. That's their color and their religion and their nationality."[2] Hugo suggests that at least some differences shouldn't be tolerated.

The religious beliefs of some members of the community put them at odds with others whose actions offend their conservative religious sensibilities—not just vampires, but also someone like Lafayette Reynolds, a gay African American man whose clothes and behavior shock his conservative neighbors. The use of the phrase "coming out of the coffin" to describe the public emergence of vampire culture suggests that vampires are similar to homosexuals in their struggle for acceptance.[3] And *True Blood*'s opening title sequence shows a billboard that converts the famous antigay slogan of Westboro Baptist Church in Topeka, "God hates fags," to "God hates fangs."

In the Southern Vampire Mysteries, Lafayette Reynolds is murdered a few pages into *Living Dead in Dallas* and discussed only in passing to illustrate Sookie's sympathy for his doubly difficult minority identity. As a major figure in the first two seasons of *True Blood*, however, Lafayette brings the issue of homosexuality into sharper focus. His expanded story line places him in direct conflict with his foil, Eric. Both are flamboyantly sexual, although with different sexual orientations. Lafayette cooks at a bar, while Eric owns a bar where no food is needed. Lafayette displays himself on the Internet for money; Eric displays himself at Fangtasia for curious fang-bangers. Big problems arise, however, when Eric imprisons Lafayette for weeks, leaving him traumatized. Superficial similarities based on the shared experience of discrimination do not necessarily make for friendship. The lesson seems to be that even two groups whose experiences are roughly parallel may find collaboration difficult.

That victims of discrimination don't always band together is evident in the fact that many of Sookie's most difficult conflicts are with other women who—in an ideal feminist world—should be her allies. Disagreements among women pose problems for a united feminist front. Sookie is often threatened by and engages in violence against other women. She fights with Maryann Forrester and Lorena on *True Blood*, and kills her romantic rival Debbie Pelt in the fourth book of the Southern

Vampire Mysteries. Economic boundaries also limit Sookie's opportunities and bother her most when she compares herself to other women, especially the ones Bill Compton dates after their breakup in the third book. As a white woman, however, Sookie has advantages that other women do not.

Consider the plight of Tara Thornton, Sookie's best friend on *True Blood*. Tara is attractive, intelligent, and fiercely independent, but also black, poor, and the daughter of an alcoholic single mother. When viewers meet Tara in the show's first episode, she's just about to quit her retail job under circumstances that illustrate the special challenges faced by black women. Tara is reading Naomi Klein's *The Shock Doctrine: The Rise of Disaster Capitalism*, a book that shows Tara to be smart and worldly. When she quits her job, she threatens to send her "baby-daddy," fresh out of jail, to kick in the teeth of her boss and the difficult customer in the store. To her horror, they take her seriously: "Oh my God! I'm not *serious*, you pathetic racist. I don't *have* a baby. Damn! I know you have to be stupid, but do you have to be that stupid?" In one simple statement, Tara breaks down a stereotype about black women. She also associates the practice of stereotyping with white people's sense of entitlement, as shown in the customer's expectation that Tara will magically produce plastic sheeting and her reference to her boss's history of ass-grabbing.

It's easy to see why Tara and Sookie are friends. They grew up together, facing similar hardships. Sookie's grandmother seems to have raised both girls. Both Sookie and Tara are intelligent women who work in service industry jobs. It makes sense that with their similar backgrounds, they would have similar roles. But Sookie has certain privileges because she is white that Tara does not. The myth of the single black mother with a violent "baby-daddy" in prison doesn't haunt Sookie, even though Arlene, another waitress at Merlotte's, comes close to being the white version of this stereotype. Could this difference be the root of Tara's defensive, quick-tempered public persona?

Is Sookie in a position to recognize the innate unfairness? After all, she gets to be the story's hero, while Tara does not.

Tara's efforts on behalf of herself and others often backfire, even when she goes after her goals with the same heroic intentions as Sookie. Tara attempts to better her life and the lives of those around her by, in the first place, trying to reconcile with her mother. In this process, however, Tara sees her mother taken over by religious enthusiasm as Tara herself succumbs to her own problems with alcohol. Landing in jail for drunk driving, she's "rescued" by Maryann, who seems to represent the possibility of a new and healthier lifestyle. Instead, Tara finds herself participating in orgies, murder, cannibalism, and pagan rituals. Her white "savior," Maryann, only enables more bad choices that wreck Tara's life and lead to her being victimized again. Tara's plight shows that racial inequalities can often complicate a black woman's attempt to achieve her full potential. In the Southern Vampire Mysteries, Tara is far less developed as a character. She's described as a high school friend of Sookie's, and her race and background are not made fully clear (although we do learn that her parents were abusive and neglectful alcoholics). *True Blood* transforms Tara's story into a reflection on a core obstacle to any united feminist agenda, the special disadvantages faced by some women on account of their race or cultural background.

Supernatural Sex

True Blood is nothing if not sexy. However, deciding whether sexual liberation is a source of empowerment or oppression for women has long been a difficult issue for feminism. Debates over sexuality—particularly about the roles of sex workers and women in pornography—became sources of deep division among women in the 1980s. Lisa Duggan, professor of social and cultural analysis at New York University, describes these "sex wars" as "a series of bitter political and cultural battles" that polarized political activists within the feminist movement.[4]

The cultural anthropologist and feminist activist Gayle Rubin explains the opposing viewpoints:

> One tendency [within feminism] has criticized the restrictions on women's sexual behavior and denounced the high costs imposed on women for being sexually active. This tradition of feminist sexual thought has called for a sexual liberation that would work for women as well as for men. The second tendency has considered sexual liberalization to be inherently a mere extension of male privilege.[5]

True Blood sends a sex-positive message, at least on the surface. The show revels in steamy love scenes, a major source of its wild popularity. Sookie's growing sexual self-confidence is a central theme of the first season, and the humorous treatment of Lafayette's prostitution and Internet pornography business recalls those two specific sources of conflict within the "sex wars" while extending the show's sexual openness beyond heterosexuality. Yet whether sexuality is a source of female empowerment seems unclear in both *True Blood* and reality.

The show's most vivid portrayal of sexuality comes with the maenad Maryann, who represents the extreme of pro-sex feminism. Her characterization recalls certain stereotypes of late-1970s feminism. On the one hand, her household in its calmer moments calls to mind the nurturing and communal mentality of feminist consciousness-raising groups. On the other hand, her rage to sacrifice Sam Merlotte fits the stereotype of the feminist as a man-eater. As Sookie's adversary, she highlights the risk that uninhibited sexuality poses to society and how it can become a source of violence between men and women. Maryann's minions blend sex and violence in their supernatural hedonism. In one episode, Tara and her boyfriend, Eggs Talley, beat each other up in a sex-charged encounter fueled by the flavor of Maryann's cannibalistic "hunter's soufflé."[6]

Ultimately, Maryann must be killed to restore order and bring peace to Bon Temps, a plot twist that suggests that wholly unregulated sexuality is dangerous.[7]

Although Maryann has the power to influence others, her worship of the Greek god Dionysus calls her female empowerment into question and hints that her brand of feminism is not as assertive as it appears. In the later episodes of the second season, Maryann reveals that her pursuit of Sam stems from her need for a "vessel" whose sacrifice will summon Dionysus into physical form. Her destabilization of Bon Temps had not been for her own immediate sexual gratification after all, but to create an attractive environment for Dionysus. By the season finale, Maryann is just a supplicant desperately trying to lure back her absent lord and husband. Gored by the horn of the bull she believes to be the god, she's willing to die happily if she can be "the vessel" for Dionysus. With its strong sexual charge, her death scene even bears a resemblance to the torture porn that is often at the center of feminist challenges to free sexual expression.

In contrast to Maryann, Sookie's more traditional sexual values allow her to define her own identity, boundaries, and relationships. Still, Sookie's outlook on love and sex is deeply ambivalent. She's involved in constant negotiations between her sexual impulses, her desire for independence, and her adherence to conventional morality. This all reflects feminism's internal debate over sexuality. At the core of the show is Sookie's growing comfort with her own sexuality in her relationship with Bill, as well as the sexual tension between her and other potential sexual partners like Sam and Eric. But at the same time she expresses anxiety about sex outside of a committed relationship. She explains her conundrum in *All Together Dead*, the seventh book of the Southern Vampire Mysteries: "I have lust. . . . Big, big lust. But I'm not a one-night-stand kind of woman."[8] Sookie's values are shaped partly by the conservative social codes that still linger in the Deep South. Tradition is not

Sookie's main challenge, however, nor is her sexual restraint simply an outdated mentality she needs to overcome. It's a product of personal reflection, as she reveals in *Definitely Dead*, the sixth book of the Southern Vampire Mysteries, where she tells the sexy weretiger Quinn, "I'm not interested in starting that up with someone who's just horny at the moment. . . . I want to be sure, if I have sex with you, that it's because you want to be around for a while and because you like me for who I am, not what I am." Sookie goes on to muse, "Maybe a million women had made approximately the same speech. I meant it as sincerely as any of those million."[9] Her self-respect demands sexual caution.

At times, Sookie's confusion about how to maintain boundaries in a romantic relationship calls the very coherence of feminist thought into question. A notable example comes when Sookie argues with Bill on a car ride to Shreveport early in *Living Dead in Dallas*. She's upset that Bill has offered to pay her shopping tab at the strip mall he owns, in her mind placing her in the degrading role of "kept woman" and turning her sexuality into a commodity. She asserts her independence by storming out of Bill's car, a bad decision that results in her being attacked by the maenad. But later Sookie suspects that her anger at Bill was irrational. After all, she resents Bill's making a large financial gift to the Bellefleur family while she has to struggle to pay her own bills, as though she wanted Bill to help her out, too. Baffled, she even wonders whether the "kept woman" fight might have been caused by supernatural influence—although Bill feels sure it wasn't. In her fight with Bill, Sookie seems committed to the belief that women need to maintain their independence in sexual relationships, but she's uncertain about what really constitutes independence. Perhaps because its implications are unclear, the "kept woman" argument is left out of *True Blood*'s depiction of this scene and replaced with a more straightforward argument about whether Sookie has the right to make decisions for herself.

Vocational Values

Where is the line between treasured lover, valued employee, and kept woman? At issue is not just sexuality, but also economic power. Feminism of the last few decades has fought to keep issues of workplace opportunity and fairness in the public eye, but the effort has not always been easy. Problems facing professional women today—glass ceilings and the lopsided division of housework in two-income families, for instance—seem less urgent than the basic access to the professional sphere addressed by earlier generations. When an event like Clarence Thomas's Supreme Court confirmation hearing brings sexual harassment into the public eye, media responses are as likely to make it the subject of humor as of serious debate. Sookie also wrestles with gender issues in the workplace and faces the difficulty of juggling the competing needs of personal and professional satisfaction.

Sookie understandably has misgivings about pursuing a romantic relationship with the man who signs her paychecks. But the deeper she delves into vampire culture, the more she discovers the near impossibility of avoiding the mix of business and pleasure. In *True Blood*'s first episode, Tara points out Sam's attraction to Sookie, who replies, "Tara! He is my boss!"[10] Sookie has drawn a clear line between work and romantic relationships, but it's challenged by ongoing sexual tension with Sam and her attraction to her new employer, Eric. Sookie's connection to Eric is deepened through job-related interaction. She begins a sexual relationship with Eric while being paid for his care in *Dead to the World*, the fourth book of the Southern Vampire Mysteries, and is forced to accept a blood bond with him to avoid serving Queen Sophie-Anne in *All Together Dead*. This unnerving scene—presented in a workplace context at the Vampire Summit—highlights Sookie's powerlessness in both her business and her romantic relationships with vampires. In this murky mixture of sex and work, Sookie resents that her professional commitment to Eric consistently limits her ability to make free choices in her love life.

These conflicts aren't limited to Sookie's relationships with men, whether human or vampire. Within the hierarchical vampire culture it's common to place sexual demands on subordinates. In *Dead and Gone*, the ninth book of the Southern Vampire Mysteries, Sookie learns from Eric's new bartender that the sheriff is considered a generous leader simply because he *doesn't* demand sexual services from anyone unwilling to give them. Female vampires blend sexual pursuit and hierarchical power as freely as their male counterparts. *True Blood*'s Sophie-Anne highlights vampires' manipulation of subordinates. In her first appearance, the queen is feeding on a human woman who is summarily dismissed when her services are no longer required. The interaction is both intimate and business-like, with a female authority figure exploiting a less powerful (but presumably willing) human. Lorena also reverses conventional gender assumptions about exploitive power relationships by using as romantic leverage against Bill her status as his maker. In contrast to female vampires like Lorena and Sophie-Anne, Eric and Bill balance personal affection and professional responsibility admirably.

Despite overturning our assumptions about which gender is usually the perpetrator and which the victim in cases of sexual harassment, Sookie's experience in the vampire world can still be compared to women's experiences in a patriarchal workplace. It's possible to interpret vampire-human interactions as a metaphor for the male-female balance of power. Yet Sookie's conflicted emotions about workplace relationships and her ongoing attraction to vampires complicate the potential of *True Blood* and the Southern Vampire Mysteries as feminist social commentary. Sookie's biggest challenge doesn't seem to be fighting oppression, but sorting out her own desires.

Sookie questions not just her romantic choices, but also whether she's really bettering her life by pursuing a taxing but well-paid career as a telepath instead of sticking with her lower-status but low-pressure job as a barmaid. In this regard she's living out one of the great controversies within contemporary feminism. Must women embrace career ambition in order to grow? Sookie wants to work because she prizes her independence and gets satisfaction from a job well done. When Eric offers to support her in *Dead and Gone*, she quickly declines. Professionalism is a source of pride for Sookie: when she meets Bill in the show's first episode, she defines herself through her job. "What are you?" Bill asks. "I'm Sookie Stackhouse," she replies. "I'm a waitress."[11] At the same time, Sookie often worries that her job at Merlotte's isn't good enough to earn the respect of others. She's torn between two career paths that offer different forms of satisfaction.

Sookie's professional confusion mirrors her story's ambiguous relationship to feminism and highlights problems of social class. Sookie's professional identity is deeply tied to her class identity as a barmaid. In *Dead and Gone* Sookie reflects on educational and professional access during a brief conversation with the new leader of the Shreveport werewolf pack, Alcide Herveaux. He mentions that the pack will raise enough money to send the orphaned *son* of the former pack leader to college. When Sookie is angered that the boy appears to be receiving preferential treatment over his sister, Alcide hastily adds that there might be enough money to educate the girl, too. Sookie immediately rethinks her reaction, though. Since the boy is a full-blooded werewolf and the girl is not, she isn't being discriminated against based on gender. Like the "kept woman" debate with Bill in *Living Dead in Dallas*, Sookie's conversation with Alcide moves toward an indictment of sexism that's quickly deflected by other concerns.

Sookie's career as a telepathic detective brings her into a high-stakes, competitive professional sphere. On *True Blood* we see her business relationship with Eric defined when she visits Fangtasia to help him question employees about embezzled money. Sookie agrees to work for him again only if he promises to turn the culprit over to the human authorities unharmed. She makes a similar demand in her negotiations with the vampire sheriff Stan in *Living Dead in Dallas*, once again attempting to mitigate the impact of the vampires' accustomed "business" strategy. But despite her attempts to protect others, her new professional role regularly thrusts her into violent conflicts, something she finds troubling even when her own violent behavior is in self-defense. In *Dead and Gone*, for example, Sookie considers that in contrast to her work as a telepathic detective, her original profession of barmaid was a nurturing one. The choice of whether to prioritize her job as barmaid or her role as telepath often comes down to a choice between relating to the world through nurturance or through conflict. Not unlike an ordinary woman deciding between a cutthroat career in business and a lower-paid but more nurturing path like education, Sookie must weigh concerns about salary and respect against other values. For many women and minorities, decisions in this area may be seen as setting precedents for others and having implications for how members of their group are viewed or come to think of themselves. Sookie is concerned more about how her choices will affect her own income and respectability, but she still struggles with anxiety about which career path best allows her to become the woman she wishes to be. Her unwillingness to choose one career over the other shows just how difficult these decisions are.

More Questions than Answers

Sookie's career paths—just like her navigation of workplace romance, her conflicted relationship to sex, and her unequal relationships to those in other marginalized groups—raise more questions than answers. Sookie faces confusing interactions and internal conflict that obscure a simple path to female empowerment. On the other hand, she demonstrates the persistence of feminist values through her demands for independence and her conscientious efforts to treat others as equals. In the end, *True Blood* offers both a critique and a celebration of contemporary feminism, never shying away from its innate complexities.

NOTES

1. See William M. Curtis's chapter in this volume, "'Honey, If We Can't Kill People, What's the Point of Being a Vampire?': Can Vampires Be Good Citizens?" for more on how the hierarchical structure of the vampire community challenges liberal political ideals like autonomy and toleration.

2. Charlaine Harris, *Living Dead in Dallas* (New York: Ace Books, 2002), p. 144.

3. See Patricia Brace and Robert Arp's chapter in this volume, "Coming Out of the Coffin and Coming Out of the Closet," for more on the comparison between vampires and homosexuals.

4. Lisa Duggan and Nan Hunter, *Sex Wars: Sexual Dissent and Political Culture* (New York: Routledge, 1995), p. 1.

5. Gayle Rubin, "Thinking Sex: Notes for a Radical Theory of the Politics of Sexuality," in *Pleasure and Danger: Exploring Female Sexuality*, ed. Carol Vance (London: Pandora, 1992), pp. 35–36.

6. Episode 208, "Timebomb."

7. For more on this plot twist and what it means, see Kevin J. Corn and George A. Dunn's chapter in this volume, "Let the Bon Temps Roll: Sacrifice, Scapegoats, and Good Times."

8. Charlaine Harris, *All Together Dead* (New York: Ace Books, 2007), p. 32

9. Charlaine Harris, *Definitely Dead* (New York: Ace Books, 2006), p. 248.

10. Episode 101, "Strange Love."

11. Ibid.

SOOKIE, SIGMUND, AND THE EDIBLE COMPLEX

Ron Hirschbein

The . . . emphasis on *Thou shalt not kill* makes it
certain that we spring from an endless ancestry of
murderers with whom the lust for killing was in the
blood, as possibly it is to this day with ourselves.

—Sigmund Freud[1]

Who is Sookie Stackhouse? Vampire Bill, an undead southern
gentleman struggling to refine his tastes, wants to know. Sookie
is wonderfully suited to his tastes, yet he's puzzled after just
one lick of her blood—she tastes different from other people.
"What are you?" Sookie usually dismisses such questions with
a self-serving response: "I'm a waitress." But, on occasion,
she reveals the truth: "What I am, is telepathic . . . I can hear
people's thoughts."[2]

However, in her electrifying encounter with Maryann
Forrester, Sookie learns that she is much more. The maenad's
supernatural powers are no match for the shocking jolt she

receives at Sookie's hands. No wonder Maryann marvels, "*What are you?*" Even Sookie is clueless, but stay tuned—ideally on your plasma TV.

The Edible Complex

We all speak Freud now, correctly or not.

—Peter Gay[3]

According to Sigmund Freud (1856–1938), the founder of psychoanalysis, we deceive ourselves if we believe we are totally in control of our lives. Our ego—the conscious self we *think* we are—is besieged by contradictory internal and external forces. We are not fully aware of these forces operating against our wills and behind our backs, since they're often unconscious. Some of these forces originate in what Freud called the id, the part of our personality that contains our instinctual drives. Initially, Freud reduced the id to sexuality and the drive to self-preservation, believing that the "pleasure principle"—and the desire for sexual pleasure in particular—motivates most of what we do. But he wound up concluding that the id, the core of our being, is actually driven by both life-affirming Eros and by death-affirming Thanatos: "I drew the conclusion that, besides the instinct to preserve living substance and to join it into larger units [Eros] there must be another contrary instinct seeking to dissolve those units and to bring them back to their primary inorganic state."[4]

In addition to the drives that originate in the id, the ego also has to contend with internalized cultural norms. Conscience and the demands of civilization comprise what Freud called the superego, a part of our personality that is largely opposed to the cravings of the id. Freud is famous, or notorious, for his theory of the Oedipus complex, the somewhat upsetting, even *icky*, idea that a young boy's id originally lusts after his mother and, as a result, secretly harbors murderous designs on his father, whom he regards as his rival. In the end, the boy realizes that pursuing a rivalry with his much more powerful Dear Old Dad isn't likely to end well for junior, so he learns to renounce his desire—the first of many unhappy renunciations to come.

Not having known any vampires, Freud didn't get a chance to speculate about the edible complex, the unrepressed desire that drives someone like Bill Compton to the taste of someone like Sookie. For most of us, the renunciation of desire demanded by civilization means that duty trumps pleasure, erotic needs become directed toward more suitable objects than Mom, and the genitals—not the oral cavity, as with vampires—become the primary or even exclusive organs of sexual pleasure. Not so for the vampire. He hears the call of Eros for a life aimed at sensual gratification.[5] And vampires violate human taboos. After all, the female vampires who seduce human men are old enough to be their mothers. But Freud didn't think such a life would ever be available to most of us. Who would do the drudgery essential for civilization if we spent all of our time and energy on sensual gratification? Thanatos, on the other hand, has its uses, such as warfare. Thanatos, in effect, seduces Eros, leading to infatuation with sexualized violence. No wonder we enjoy *True Blood*.

As Freud explains our dilemma, civilization would perish if people did what comes naturally, but the repression of our instincts demanded by civilization leads to our not-so-quiet lives of despair.[6]

Sookie and Sigmund experience these discontents. They realize, to paraphrase Sigmund, that civilization gives us everything except happiness. They also share uncanny powers, reading minds (more in a moment on how Sigmund does that) and witnessing the strange power of posthypnotic suggestion, otherwise known as "glamouring." Both Sookie and Sigmund know that people have little control over their lives, and they sometimes discover more than they care to know about other people. Finally, Sookie actualizes what Freud thought eluded most people, a fully developed erotic life. But she is also painfully aware of the truth behind his lamentation that "we are never so defenseless against suffering as when we love, never so helplessly unhappy as when we have lost our love object."[7]

Bon Temps and Its Discontents

> Our fellow citizens have not sunk so low as we feared because they have never risen as high as we believed.
>
> —Sigmund Freud[8]

A realistic portrayal of Bon Temps would bore us to death: relentless hours of mind-numbing routine punctuated by a few Saturday night guilty pleasures. How might citizens cope? Sookie's friend Tara Thornton might read self-help books such as Norman Vincent Peale's ever-popular *Power of Positive Thinking*, with its teaching that an attitude adjustment is all it takes to be happy—the glass is half-full, not half-empty.[9]

Freud wouldn't buy it, nor ultimately would Tara. They know that their discontents aren't merely a matter of a bad attitude. They're realists. I can hear Tara exclaiming, "Gimme a break! Yeah right! I'll put a happy face on my abusive, alcoholic mother. What's wrong with me? Racism doesn't make me happy; I'm not even wild about sexism and zero job prospects." Freud's prognosis resonates: "The best we can hope for is to change hysterical misery to ordinary unhappiness."[10]

Civilization—or a modicum of security—demands the renunciation of instinctive gratification. We can't do what comes naturally. But we pay a terrible emotional price for the tenuous security of civilization. Long repressed passions ferment into intoxicating pathologies. But in the meantime, life goes on. Sam Merlotte slings burgers, Jason Stackhouse labors on the road crew, the chip on Tara's shoulder grows bigger, and Sookie grows old and arthritic from waiting tables. Those who don't die of boredom are taken by old age or by Sam's cheeseburgers. But routine isn't the stuff of primetime.

True Blood is a Freudian fable: a saga of our species doing what comes naturally. But when Freud talks about gratifying the id, he means something more than the cheap thrills of drinking and womanizing. These pleasures are, at best, tame surrogates for the incendiary, all-consuming gratification we crave. In season 2 the good folk of Bon Temps discover what the undead, the V junkies, and Maryann already know: feeble watered-down pleasures can't compare with the ecstasy of full-throated instinctual gratification. There's nothing feeble about the signature features of *True Blood*, convulsive sex and violence. Sigmund and Maryann agree: "The feeling of happiness derived from the satisfaction of a wild, instinctual impulse untamed by the ego is incomparably more intense than that derived from sating an instinct that has been tamed."[11]

Nothing New under the Moon

Few folkloric creations have survived for so long [as vampire myths] in such diverse cultural and geographic situations. There must be something common to human nature to create such universality and endurance. A Freudian interpretation of the myth can uncover such a bond.

—Laura Collopy[12]

In the world according to Freud, vampire myths are universal because they reflect what's universal in us—*primal instincts* and *defense mechanisms*. The vampire is the avatar of repressed erotic and destructive passions, and (as we'll see) also an enabler of defense mechanisms such as projection and denial.

First, *True Blood* vampires are able to give free expression to their ids, while overcoming what Freud deemed the perennial sources of human misery:

We are threatened with suffering from three directions: from our own body which is doomed to decay and

dissolution, and cannot do it without pain and anxiety ...
from the external world which may rage against us with
overwhelming and merciless forces of destruction, and
finally from our relations with other men.[13]

Let's look how vampires overcome each of these sources of
suffering in turn:

- *Our feeble, mortal bodies.* Bill flies to Sookie's aid to save
  her from imminent death. All it takes is just a few drops of
  his blood—and no aggravation with insurance companies.
  Vampires also enjoy a conditional immortality, conditional
  inasmuch as they can die only from external causes. Godric's
  two-thousand-year life span tops our proverbial three-score-
  and-ten. Vampires are to die for!
- *Nature and the external world.* Vampires don't age. Godric
  still looks peppy after two thousand years. Some even defy
  gravity by flying from place to place. Their magical strength
  overcomes nature—because it's supernatural.
- *Social relations.* Before coming out of the coffin, vampires
  were relatively untroubled by human beings, except for rare
  occasions when they would perish at the hands of someone who had a stake in their destinies. Vampires seduced
  human beings, then drained and discarded them. No worries. Human beings were a thing to be used—as the more
  wicked *True Blood* vampires *believe* they should still be today.
  For Vampire Bill, however, this is all *so* fifteenth-century.
  But his struggle to mainstream leaves him vulnerable to the
  misery Freud predicted as the fate of all civilized beings. Bill
  is despised, unjustly accused, and tormented by the bitter-
  sweet vagaries of romance. Still, there's much to envy in his
  existence. Even if things go awry, Bill may still be around in
  2110 to find another Sookie.

But despite the way vampires fulfill our fantasy of gratifying our primal instincts in an existence that has overcome the

perennial sources of human suffering—or maybe because they do—they also make ideal villains. Vampire myths reveal the workings of the commonplace defense mechanisms known as projection and denial. We deny our unacceptable passions by projecting them onto a scapegoat.[14] Truth be told, there's lots of emotional garbage to dump onto others. As Freud explains,

> Men are not [simply] gentle creatures who want to be loved. . . . Their neighbor [whom they are commanded to love] tempts them to satisfy their aggressiveness on him, to exploit his capacity for work without compensation, to use him sexually without his consent, to seize his possessions, to humiliate him, to cause him pain, to torture and kill him.[15]

These ineradicable, savage passions reflect our biological heritage. Freud points out that the Ten Commandments don't simply reflect a higher morality. On the contrary, they reveal our authentic desires. "What no human soul desires stands in no need of prohibition; it is excluded automatically."[16] Vampires provide screens onto which we can project our unthinkable thoughts and perverse desires. They blaspheme, disrespect parents, covet their neighbors, and kill. Freud thinks that deep down, at the core of our being, we all secretly wish we could do the same—we're all public enemies, enemies of civilized morality, he quips. Just as we can't vanquish these desires that constitute what we detest in ourselves, we can't readily kill vampires since they are simply the projection of all those parts of ourselves that we wish to disown. Sookie and Sigmund know more than they care to about this savage heritage. They read minds.

Sookie's and Sigmund's Gift

Sookie is essentially different, since she's telepathic. When I established Sookie's character, it seemed to me

that she would only date a certain kind of vampire, one
that appealed to her in a down-home kind of way . . . the
kind of fellow she could relate to.

—Charlaine Harris[17]

Sookie reads minds—plain and simple. She taps directly into
the unconscious. Freud gained access to unthinkable thoughts
and passions through a journey that began with hypnosis—
glamouring in vampire parlance—and ended with the laying on
of hands. But Sookie and Sigmund both come to the same conclusions: their neighbors are obsessed with sexualized violence.

Working with his mentor Josef Breuer (1842–1925), Freud
witnessed how posthypnotic suggestion operates. A subject under
hypnosis is given a command to perform upon waking, such as
dancing around the room. Freud observed that under "posthypnotic suggestion, a command given under the spell is slav-
ishly carried out subsequently in the normal state."[18] Subjects
perform as commanded but recall nothing about what happened
while under hypnosis. They're unaware of the forces governing
their behavior, which are *unconscious*. If asked to account for their
peculiar behavior of, for instance, dancing around the room, they
rationalize, inventing convincing reasons for their behavior, but
remaining clueless about the real reasons.

In observing posthypnotic suggestion, Freud came to recognize the awesome power of the unconscious: "If an innocuous
command given in a trance results in peculiar behavior, imagine
the power of childhood traumas. The fixation of mental life to
pathogenic trauma is one of the most significant characteristics
of neurosis."[19]

Freud believed that neurotic symptoms originated from
repressed memories of childhood traumas and that psycho-
analysis could uncover these memories. Sigmund abandoned
hypnosis for psychoanalysis because he wasn't good at hypnosis
and he believed patients needed to participate consciously in
their own recovery. Freud turned instead to the laying on of

hands. In *the* iconic Freudian vision, we see the patient lying on the couch while the Father of Psychoanalysis lays hands on the patient's forehead and encourages free association to reveal the repressed trauma that has made the patient sick.[20]

True Blood aims at entertainment, not therapy, but it doesn't let us forget that we're governed by primal instincts. Sookie and Sigmund both know their neighbors are obsessed and tormented by unexpressed impulses, fantasies, and memories they desperately struggle to repress. Reading customers' minds doesn't renew Sookie's faith in humanity. Their secret thoughts, even the unrepressed ones, are seldom benign. Men think of Sookie as a sex object, and women gossip about her odd behavior and attraction to vampires. In the very first episode, Sookie saves Bill when she reads the minds of the Rattrays, evildoers bent on draining Bill and selling his blood.

Consequently, Sookie regards her gift as a disability. Dating is a disaster. She knows her dates' secrets—they have posterior motives. Worse still, she breaks down at Gran's wake after listening to the cacophony of neighbors casting aspersions upon her. Ordinarily she deals with her "disability" with weary resignation, but sometimes it's too much. Bill, of course, is particularly attractive—because she can't read his mind.

Mind reading also demoralized Freud, especially in the aftermath of World War I. He lamented that "[n]o event has ever destroyed so much that is precious in the common possessions of humanity, confused so many of the clearest intelligence, or so thoroughly debased what is highest."[21] No longer preoccupied with the notion that all suffering is rooted in repressed sexuality, he began to stress the primal instinct of Thanatos, the death drive, a pure wish for destruction that he believed originally aimed at one's own death but could be directed outward toward others when it encountered resistance from our instinct of self-preservation.

Sookie and Sigmund realize that both the living and the undead often kill over trivialities. Vampires kill human beings for pleasure or when they outlive their usefulness. Human beings are no better, as Bill reminds Sookie. The good people of Bon Temps kill—or wish they could kill—their brethren merely for cavorting with vampires or to repay insults, real or imagined. As if commenting on scenes in *True Blood*, Freud wrote: "Our unconscious will murder for trifles; like the ancient, Athenian Law of Draco, it knows no other punishment . . . Death. . . . Every injury to our almighty and autocratic ego is at bottom a crime of *lese-majeste*."[22]

True Blood is about a world out of control in which the center no longer holds. Not that human beings object to losing control, as the Maryann story line makes clear. Maryann provides occasion for *the* supreme pleasure, the chance to be out of control. "Control," she tells Tara and Eggs Talley, Tara's lover, "is just a cage this stupid culture uses to lock up who we really are. We need to be out of control. We crave it."[23] And so, consumed by that pent-up "wild instinctive impulse untamed by the ego," Bon Temps goes berserk with sexualized violence enabled by Maryann.[24]

Speaking of enablers, Vampire Bill's deadly embrace makes it possible for Jessica, the pious ingenue, to do what comes naturally. She put the "vamp" in vampire—what a pain in the neck for prospective mother-in-law Maxine! And, in a grand mal catharsis, Jessica lets loose long suppressed human desires: she attacks dear ol' dad—revenge is best served hot!

Love at First Bite

A small minority [is] enabled by their constitution to find happiness, in spite of everything, along the path of love. . . . These people make themselves independent of their object's acquiescence by displacing what they mainly value from being loved on to loving.

—Sigmund Freud[25]

Some of Freud's later followers indicted their master's notion of "genital tyranny," his account of how in the course of what he took to be normal psychosexual development the child's sexual impulses become entirely subordinated to the genitals.[26] The philosopher Herbert Marcuse (1898–1979) argued that far from being natural or inevitable, "genital tyranny" reflected the way that a repressive society mobilizes almost the entire body for alienated labor, with only the genitals remaining as instruments of gratification.[27] Working-class womanizer Jason Stackhouse might be considered a prime example of the consequences of this repression. Marcuse wanted to reverse the process of "genital tyranny" so we could return to the "polymorphous perversity" of the infant, who Freud believed could derive sexual pleasure from any part of the body.

But Freud himself pointed toward a very different path to happiness: redirecting erotic energy "away from its sexual aims and transforming the instinct into an impulse with an *inhibited aim*."[28] The rare individual Freud has in mind has not only inhibited (or sublimated) the desire for sexual gratification that is the original aim of our erotic impulses, but has also ascended from the love for particular individuals to affection for all humanity. The happiness of such individuals is a result of their sublimation of erotic energies through which they "bring about in themselves . . . a state of evenly suspended, steadfast, affectionate feeling that has little external resemblance to the stormy agitations of genital love, from which it is nonetheless derived."[29] Sookie doesn't perfectly realize this ideal, since she remains a sexual being intensely fixated on Bill, but she nonetheless risks everything for friends *and* enemies—even loathsome Eric Northman—in a way that somewhat resembles someone else who really did sublimate his love into an affection for all human beings and, just like Sookie, even for many nonhumans as well.

Freud, no champion of Catholicism, offers a surprising choice for his exemplar of sublimated love: "Perhaps St. Francis of Assisi went furthest in thus exploiting love for the benefit of an inner feeling of happiness."[30] Sickened by war, Francis (ca. 1182–1226) returned from the Crusades, renounced his patrimony, and devoted his life to expressing unconditional affection toward all humanity and nature. Francis had the solace of a belief in immortality, a comfort that eludes many in secular culture. And yet, as Freud argues, our own death is unimaginable; unconsciously, we believe in our own immortality. No wonder we identify with the death-defying, immortal characters of *True Blood*!

NOTES

1. Sigmund Freud, "Thoughts on War and Death," in *On Creativity and the Unconscious*, ed. Benjamin Nelson (New York: Harper & Row, 1958), p. 230.

2. Charlaine Harris, *Dead until Dark* (New York: Ace Books, 2001), p. 32.

3. Peter Gay, "Sigmund Freud: A Brief Life," in Freud, *Civilization and Its Discontents*, trans. James Strachey (New York: W.W. Norton, 1961), p. ix.

4. Ibid., p. 77

5. Neo-Freudians such as Herbert Marcuse explore the radical implications of Eros in works such as *Eros and Civilization* (Boston: Beacon Press, 1955).

6. As the title suggests, that is the conclusion of *Civilization and Its Discontents*.

7. Gay, "Sigmund Freud," p. 33.

8. Freud, "Thoughts on War and Death," p. 213.

9. Norman Vincent Peale, *The Power of Positive Thinking* (New York: Prentice Hall, 1952).

10. Sigmund Freud, *Studies in Hysteria* (New York: Penguin, 2004), p. 307.

11. Ibid., p. 29.

12. Laura Collopy, "A Freudian Interpretation of the Vampire Myth," in *Vampire Junction*, www.afn.org/~vampires/myth.html.

13. Gay, "Sigmund Freud," p.26.

14. For more on scapegoating, see Kevin J. Corn and George A. Dunn's chapter in this volume, "Let the Bon Temps Roll: Sacrifice, Scapegoats, and Good Times."

15. Freud, "Thoughts on War and Death," p. 214.

16. Sigmund Freud, *The Standard Edition of the Complete Psychological Works of Sigmund Freud*, ed. by Carrie Lee Rothgeb (New York: International Universities Press, 1973), vol. 14, p. 296.

17. Charlaine Harris's Official Web site, www.charlaineharris.com.

18. Sigmund Freud, *Five Lectures On Psycho-Analysis*, trans. James Strachey (New York: W.W. Norton, 1977), p. 19.

19. Ibid., p. 17.

20. See "Lecture 4" in *Five Lectures on Psycho-Analysis* for an account of Freud's abandonment of hypnosis in favor of the psychoanalysis.

21. Freud, *The Standard Edition of the Complete Psychological Works of Sigmund Freud* vol. 14, p. 275.

22. Ibid., p. 232.

23. Episode 209, "I Will Rise Up." London's Freud Museum contains one of Freud's prize possessions: an Etruscan vessel depicting the face of a maenad. See www.freud.org.uk/about/collections/detail/10148/.

24. Gay, "Sigmund Freud," p. 29.

25. Ibid., p. 56

26. See Yiannis Gabriel, *Freud and Society* (Boston: Routledge and Kegan, 1983), pp. 200–204.

27. See Herbert Marcuse, *Eros and Civilization: A Philosophic Inquiry Into Freud* (Boston: Beacon Press, 1966), pp. 181–187. See also Gabriel, *Freud and Society*, pp. 200–204.

28. Gay, "Sigmund Freud," p. 57.

29. Ibid.

30. Ibid.

PART FOUR

"I AM ACTUALLY OLDER THAN YOUR JESUS": NATURAL, SUPERNATURAL, AND DIVINE

LET THE BON TEMPS ROLL

Sacrifice, Scapegoats, and Good Times

Kevin J. Corn and George A. Dunn

A lot of people had been doing some very bad things. The citizens of Bon Temps could see the ransacked buildings and the fresh graffiti, not to mention their own underwear strewn willy-nilly in the streets. They could see and *smell* a large tree upholstered with rotting meat. They could feel the aches from bruises, broken bones, and the odd missing finger. Also missing were most of their memories. Of course, we the viewers of *True Blood* know exactly what brought all this to pass. We saw the townspeople swept up in a wave of pandemonium, convinced that it was their religious duty to let the good times roll. We saw them indulge every passion and act on every dark desire, as their parties erupted in ecstatic orgies that sought their climax in human sacrifice. We saw them become uninhibited devotees of Dionysus, god of wine, revelry, madness, and (incidentally) dismemberment. And, of course, we saw just what goes into a "hunter's soufflé."

Of Scapegoats, Sausages, and "Eggs"

"Used to be they all thought I was crazy. Now they know I'm telling the truth and they can't face it. Zombie-eyed freaks!"

—Andy Bellefleur[1]

With only a few exceptions, the participants in this mayhem had no memories of what happened or the parts they played in it. A convenient collective amnesia gripped Bon Temps. Of course, that doesn't prevent some of the more fertile local imaginations from filling in those memory gaps with wild speculations. Rumor has it that Maryann Forrester—whom everyone seems eager to blame for reasons that may be unrelated to her actual guilt—was really an alien ("Maryann Forrester rhymes with Martian foreigner") or possibly "an agent of the pharmaceutical companies and the liberal media," who "poisoned our water supply with LSD as a mind control experiment."[2] Sam Merlotte is one of a small number of Bon Temps residents who know the truth, but he's not telling. Instead, he has concocted a cover story, every bit as fictional as those other accounts, even if a bit more prosaic and plausible. He confides in the local busybodies ("just between you and me") that the whole town was the victim of a bad batch of vodka ("pure ethanol") from a distillery over in Breaux Bridge.

Space aliens, pharmaceutical companies, the liberal media, Maryann, and Breaux Bridge distillers are all candidates for what the contemporary scholar René Girard (about whom we'll be hearing more shortly) calls a *scapegoat*, an outsider who bears the blame for our troubles, so that we don't have to blame ourselves or one another. The scapegoat, as we'll see shortly, is the bringer of peace and harmony to communities and individuals, a peace that comes from deflecting painful feelings of guilt, resentment, and hostility onto someone other than ourselves and our neighbors.

Sam clearly appreciates the wisdom of keeping the truth hidden. But even more important, he recognizes the need to explain the collapse of Bon Temps' social order and shift the blame from its permanent residents. Indeed, his lie was a gift that allowed them to go on seeing themselves as fine upstanding citizens. Needless to say, they can't move forward without some explanation of this traumatic interruption of the normal course of events. But the naked truth—that it was their own libidinous and aggressive urges run amok—would be a little too painful for them to seriously consider. Andy Bellefleur discovers this problem with the truth when he confronts Jane Bodehouse with certain facts concerning her severed finger and gets repaid for his trouble with derisive laughter. Of course, Andy's motive isn't a dispassionate pursuit of truth, either, but rather a desire to be vindicated and lauded as a hero. His interest in truth is compromised by vanity in the same way his neighbors' vanity permits them to swallow falsehoods. And Andy's enthusiasm for full disclosure would probably diminish considerably if he were to recall how he also joined the ranks of the "zombie-eyed freaks" and participated in the aborted sacrifice of Sam Merlotte. As Lafayette Reynolds tells Sookie Stackhouse, "I don't think it's healthy for a motherfucker to know everything he done done. It's like knowing what's in the sausage. Just eat it. Enjoy it."[3]

Lafayette's suspicion that knowing the truth may not always have salutary repercussions was shared by the philosopher Friedrich Nietzsche (1844–1900). Nietzsche believed that the "basic will of the [mind or] spirit" wasn't necessarily the will to truth, but rather the drive to interpret the world and our experiences in a way that renders them coherent and manageable. The mind "wants to be master in and around its own house and wants to feel that it is master."[4] In other words, we're driven to interpret the world in ways that enhance our sense of control over our lives and bolster our self-esteem. Sometimes this "basic will" favors discovery of the truth, but not always. In a brief aphorism, Nietzsche sums up how the truth often becomes a casualty of more pressing psychological needs: "'I have done that,' says my memory. 'I cannot have done that says my pride,' and remains inexorable. Eventually— memory yields."[5]

Of course, the amnesia suffered by the residents of Bon Temps *seems* to be involuntary to a much greater extent than the pride-induced forgetfulness described in Nietzsche's scenario. At least, that's the impression produced by a suggestive special effect employed by the producers of *True Blood* throughout the second season. To show which characters were under Maryann's supernatural spell, their eyes were entirely blacked out, implying that the spell had made them blind to what they were doing. But regardless of whether the cause of their blindness and resulting amnesia was internal or external, the psychological well-being and self-esteem of most residents of Bon Temps seem to have been well served by their ignorance of "what's in the sausage"—or the hunter's soufflé.

The exception who proves the rule is "Eggs" Benedict Talley. After Maryann's demise, he's the only person alive who had been in her entourage before she came to Bon Temps. It was Eggs who actually wielded the knife on Miss Jeanette, Daphne Landry, and Sam. But he differs from others in Bon Temps in a more significant way: after a misspent youth that earned him some time in prison, Eggs made a conscious decision to accept the consequences of his past mistakes and take his life in a new direction. As he tells Sookie, "I did a lot of terrible things in my past, but I paid for them." Assuming responsibility for his actions sets him apart from most residents of Bon Temps. So when he discovers blood on his hands after waking up from his most recent "blackout," he doesn't automatically look for someone else to blame, even after Sookie pleads with him not to blame himself. Eggs implores her to help him recover his lost memories, however horrible they may be. Sobbing, he exclaims, "I can't live with myself not knowing what

I did." Contrary to Nietzsche, Eggs's pride doesn't push him to bury his traumatic memories but rather to try to exhume them, with devastating psychological consequences.

Why didn't the usual mechanisms of repression work for Eggs? Why was he unable to put the past behind him, forget it, and move forward with his life? It could be that the others had a community life to which they could return and that allowed them to reinforce one another in the whole project of forgetting. Or it could just be that this ex-con was actually a man of much greater honesty and integrity than the others. Either way, the guilt he experienced was so intense that it destroyed him. Eggs's tragic end illustrates why the option of seeking a scapegoat is so attractive. His shattered psychological wholeness presents in miniature what can happen to an entire community when blame and acrimony can't be channeled outside.

The Dionysian Pack Mentality

> Madness is rare among individuals—but in groups, parties, nations, and ages, it is the rule.
>
> —Friedrich Nietzsche[6]

When Nietzsche spoke of the madness that seizes human beings in "parties," he wasn't referring to the wild soirees hosted by Maryann, but he easily could have been. In a 2009 interview, Michelle Forbes, the actress who played Maryann, stated that the producers of *True Blood* used the show's second season to create a "landscape" for "allegorically" exploring, among other themes, "pack mentality thinking"—a form of madness that leaves us prone to commit certain evils in groups that we might never consider committing as individuals.[7] Clearly, the producer Alan Ball is pushing into some very serious territory. Ever since World War II, with concerns raised by the Holocaust, a broad cultural discussion of *pack mentality*, *mob psychology*, and *group-think* has attempted to illuminate such phenomena as genocide and the roots of racism, hatred, war, and even religion. But, as Nietzsche shows us, philosophers had already been reflecting on this phenomenon for a long time.

One of the first philosophers to describe the pack mentality was Plato (427–347 B.C.E.), who used a striking image to depict the power that any large assembly tends to exercise over its members. Plato observed that as any assembled group begins loudly and vehemently praising or blaming anything, "the rocks and the very place surrounding them echo and redouble the uproar of blame and praise."[8] Through this image of an emotional contagion so irresistible that even inanimate objects are swept up in its sway, Plato highlights our own all-too-human susceptibility to the influence of the crowd, which he suggests can reduce us to mindless objects that reflexively absorb and echo the feelings of those who surround us. Carried on the tide of some powerful group emotion, who would "not be swept away by such blame and praise and go, borne by the flood, wherever it tends so that he'll say the same things are noble and base as they do, practice what they practice, and be such as they are?"[9]

Plato was thinking primarily of people gathered in political assemblies or at public theatrical performances, but he could just as well be describing what happens at Maryann's parties, as everyone seems to leave their capacity for independent judgment at the door, along with most of their clothing. Of course, the series depicts those revelers as having succumbed to a spell cast by a maenad with supernatural powers. But when we recall what Forbes said about *True Blood*'s "allegorical" exploration of the "pack mentality" theme, it's hard not to recognize that Maryann's maenadic spell works as a metaphor for the very real way people become possessed by whatever powerful mood or intention has gripped the rest of the crowd. Leaving aside Maryann's supernatural powers, the entirely *natural* tendency of people to surrender the reins of their conscience to the group goes a long way toward explaining how she was able to get the good people of Bon Temps to throw restraint to the wind and indulge their most outrageous passions.

It's no accident that this avatar of the pack mentality is also a devotee of the god Dionysus. The Greek god Dionysus, known to the Romans as Bacchus, was a popular deity throughout the ancient Mediterranean world. When Queen Sophie-Anne of Louisiana described the ancient cult of Dionysus as one "that encourages you to get hammered, run naked through the woods, have sex with whoever, whatever, and it's all part of getting closer to God," she wasn't far off the mark.[10] We could describe Dionysus as the patron deity of sex, drugs, and rock 'n' roll. (Wherever two or three thousand are gathered together in a mosh pit, he will be present among them.) He was a rock star among Greece's classical divinities, frequently portrayed with a retinue of frenzied groupies known as maenads—wild, god-intoxicated women, whose worship services typically involved dancing, uninhibited sexual antics, dismembering live animals (and sometimes even men), and devouring their victims' flesh. Festivals held in honor of Dionysus, known in Rome as Bacchanalia, may not have always gone quite that far, but drunken debauchery seems to have been the order of the day. Traces of these ancient festivals survive into modern times in wild carnivals like Mardi Gras held each year in New Orleans. (Just watch *Girls Gone Wild: New Orleans* to get a sense.) As we witness the descent of Bon Temps into the darkest depths of wild whoop-de-doo, we're struck with how fitting it is that a town that is so susceptible to Maryann's Dionysian spell should take its name from the cry that thunders through the streets each year during Mardi Gras: "Laissez les bons temps rouler!"—"Let the good times roll!"[11]

In *The Birth of Tragedy* Nietzsche wrote about the cult of Dionysus, contrasting this god of intoxication and revelry with Apollo, the god of reason, daylight, and decorum. Nietzsche associated Apollo with the *principium individuationis*, or principle of individuation. This principle, which has a long history in philosophy, boils down to the fairly simple idea that our world consists of distinct individuals with more or less definite boundaries marking them off from one another. You are you, a unique and unrepeatable individual, distinct from me and everyone else, however much we may outwardly resemble one another. Or at least that's how the Greeks experienced reality in the sober daylight of the god Apollo. But, according to Nietzsche, the nocturnal revelries of Dionysus told a different story. In the course of the god's orgiastic rites, his devotees would lose all sense of existing as separate and distinct individuals, as they were filled with "the blissful ecstasy that wells from the innermost depths of man, indeed of nature, at this collapse of the *principium individuationis*." As the revelers surrender to what they experience as the undifferentiated ground of their being, blissful "Dionysian emotions awake, and as they grow in intensity everything subjective vanishes into complete self-forgetfulness."[12]

Daphne Landry, the shapeshifting waitress who doubles as a covert agent for Maryann, supplies a nice description of how the devotees of Dionysus experience this ground of being: "It's really just a kind of energy. Wild energy, like lust, anger, excess, violence. Basically all the fun stuff."[13] As Daphne's description indicates, this encounter with the primal energy of life occurs in a purely emotional register, not on the level of well-defined ideas that can be contemplated in the state of calm detachment that Nietzsche associated with Apollo. The "I" that would engage in this contemplation is dissolved into the "wild energy" that flows all around and through it, an energy that is conducted through the group by that same power of emotional contagion that Plato had described. One moves to the currents of that wild energy, released from the burden of reflection that normally interposes itself between our impulses and our actions. After watching season 2 of *True Blood*, we have no trouble recognizing the attractions of this loss of self, as well as its dangers.

Zigmunt Bauman, a contemporary social theorist whose insightful description of how people act in crowds could be a firsthand account of one of Maryann's parties, writes, "In the crowd we are all alike. We go about together, we dance together, we punch together, we burn together, we kill together."[14] As we'll soon see, there's a very good reason this list of things that people do together concludes with homicide. In the meantime, Bauman identifies precisely what makes this sort of "togetherness" so appealing: "'What to do' is no more a *problem*. The target is immediately *obvious*—crystal-clear, readable in the eyes, gestures and movements of *everybody* around. Just do what others do. Not because what they do is sensible, useful, beautiful or right, or because they say so, or because you think so—but because they do it."[15]

The crowd offers us not only the excitement of riding a wild crest of shared emotion but also sweet release from the burden of having to make decisions for ourselves. It's no wonder that Maxine Fortenberry is so eager to escape the protective custody of her son, Hoyt, and get swallowed up in the crowd.

Scapegoats We Can Sink Our Teeth Into

Violence is not to be denied, but it can be diverted to another object, something it can sink its teeth into.

—René Girard[16]

The two phenomena we've been discussing—scapegoating and the pack mentality—are united in a powerful way in the writings of René Girard, whose work over the past thirty years has made the term *scapegoat* an essential feature in contemporary discussions of ethics, theology, ethnology, and literature. Girard has also given us a way to understand the pack mentality through his theory of how *mimesis*, or imitation, shapes relationships with others, both generating conflicts and helping us to resolve them. As we'll see, these ideas illuminate much of what occurs in *True Blood*, as well as in our own society.

When Girard states that human beings are *mimetic*, or imitative, creatures, he doesn't just mean that we tend to fall in line with the opinions of the crowd, praising and blaming in unison, as Plato described. He also means we are prone to another—and paradoxically more divisive—form of imitation called *mimetic desire*, the desire to obtain for ourselves what other people have, which could be some concrete item, another person's affection, or a certain status in the community. Desire is as contagious as any other emotion. But while other shared emotions tend to unite us, mimetic desire turns us into rivals when the desired object is something that can't be easily shared. Since the chief obstacle to obtaining what we desire is that someone else already has it, our relationships often become poisoned with feelings of envy and resentment that fester until something happens to cause them to erupt in open conflict.

The extent to which envy and resentment twist and torment the human soul—sometimes curdling inside as self-loathing, sometimes threatening to spew outward as violence—is no secret to Sookie Stackhouse, the telepathic waitress at Merlotte's Bar and Grill. The underside of Bon Temps society is on display for her every night, as she becomes our guide to the unspoken desires and resentments of the townspeople. Bombarded constantly with the thoughts of those around her, she frequently perceives them as a mass of dark resentments directed against anyone who is different, including herself. And this way of doling out animosity illustrates another of Girard's insights: the immediate target of our acrimony is often unrelated to the actual cause of our discontent or unhappiness.

We're all familiar with "kick the dog syndrome." Someone who has been dumped on all day at work carries his resentment home and kicks the dog or yells at the kids. Anger demands an outlet and will invent reasons to justify unloading itself on whoever happens to be available. As Girard explains, "When unappeased, violence seeks and always finds a surrogate victim. The creature that excited its fury is abruptly replaced by another, chosen only because it is vulnerable and close to hand."[17] Consider Drew Marshall. Enraged by his sister Cindy's relationship with a vampire—perhaps because he felt it was some kind of personal insult or humiliation—he murders her. But as his anger remained unabated after just one murder, he assumed a new identity as Rene Lenier, seemingly a gentle Cajun man but actually a raging serial killer who was slaying fang-bangers as an outlet for his unappeased wrath.

We witness a similar transference of resentment during and after the group session led by Sarah Newlin at the Fellowship of the Sun compound. Missy, a young girl whose neck and chest (dotted with puncture wounds) identify her as a recovering fang-banger, tearfully reports to the group how her vampire lover had treated her as "nothing but his living, breathing snack machine." Jason Stackhouse initially dismisses Sarah's suggestion that all vampires are like that and struts out of the session. But she follows him outside and, by playing on his still-raw grief and guilt over the murders of his grandmother and his girlfriend, brings him around to her point of view. Sarah turns out to be an adroit manipulator of Jason's emotions, drawing his rage away from himself and Drew Marshall and redirecting it at the vampire population with her contention that if their "kind never existed, the people you love would still be alive." As an argument for blaming every single vampire for the deaths of Gran and Amy Burley, this is a terrible piece of reasoning. But we can be fairly certain that it's not Sarah's *logic* that wins Jason over. She confides that she also lost a loved one, her sister, in what she is certain was vampiric foul play. Inviting Jason into a fellowship based on a sense of shared grievance against a perceived common enemy, Sarah tells him in a voice choked with emotion, "They stole my sister, Jason, the same way they stole your girlfriend and your grandmother."[18]

By identifying with his grief, she encourages him to identify with her in *blaming*.

The basic recruitment strategy of the Fellowship of the Sun is on full display in this scene. The trick is to persuade people like Jason that whatever their grievances might be, their real enemy is the same as the Fellowship's—the vampire community. Girard's theory helps explain why that's not difficult to do. It's our nature, he argues, not only to imitate our neighbors' *acquisitive gestures* by reaching out to grab what they grab, but also to imitate their *accusative gestures* by pointing the finger of blame in the same direction as all the fingers around us. Moreover, the gravitational pull of mimesis ensures that in a crisis it won't be long before all or most of those fingers will be pointing in the same direction, at some individual or group that Girard calls the *scapegoat*.

This *scapegoat mechanism* is the most tried and true method that communities have for dealing with the crises that arise when ongoing conflicts and mounting resentments reach a tipping point that threatens to tear the community apart in a free-for-all of reciprocal blame and recrimination. We saw how Eggs self-destructed when he was unable to purge himself of guilt and project the blame outside himself. Similarly, whole communities may come to ruin if they are unable to staunch internal conflicts by redirecting everyone's hostility away from one another—and outward toward a scapegoat. But if we can all agree to blame someone either outside the community or only marginally associated with it, rather than venting our rage on one another, we can experience the exhilarating togetherness that Bauman describes: punching together, burning together, and even killing together. The pack mentality comes to our rescue, dissolving our differences in a powerful bond of solidarity that unfortunately turns us into cruel persecutors, often of some entirely innocent person. Of course, as Girard points out, it's vital to the success of the scapegoat mechanism that we not realize what we're doing, that we really believe in the guilt of the scapegoat and remain blind to our own injustice. As Lafayette might put it, the scapegoat mechanism works only if we don't know what's in the sausage.

Because our scapegoats are blamed for problems created by all of us, they must in some way resemble us, the majority population. But they also need to bear some conspicuous difference that can act as a lightning rod to draw all of the community's accusations their way. The best scapegoats are peripheral members of the community who lack the sort of status or connections that would protect them from persecution. Our history provides us with a shameful roster of examples— Jews, gypsies, African Americans, homosexuals, immigrants, "witches," and the mentally ill ("demonically possessed") have all at various times been scapegoated for an assortment of social ills.[19] But in the world of *True Blood*, the vampire community offers the ideal scapegoat, one that the community's accumulated resentment and hostility can (to quote the epigraph from Girard that opens this section) "sink its teeth into" with gusto.[20] Vampires were once human and retain much of their original human appearance. But then there are all of those little differences that set them apart. Their skin is a bit pale. They have fangs. They burst into flame when exposed to sunlight. And, of course, let's not forget that they've spent the past several thousand years as serial killers victimizing human beings. Finally, as we're reminded by the "God hates fangs" sign that appears in the opening credit sequence, if you really want to scapegoat someone with passion and commitment, nothing can embolden your hatred quite as well as the belief that God hates them too.

The God Who ~~Comes~~ Forgives

We do not have to accuse our neighbor; we can learn to forgive him instead.

—René Girard[21]

True Blood depicts a world in which scapegoating is the norm. Because we often sympathize with its victims on the show, it's easy for us to recognize the operation of the scapegoat mechanism in the world that Alan Ball and his team has crafted for our entertainment. But it's more difficult—even downright disheartening—to accept the idea that this enchanted, fascinating, and grotesque world might actually reflect our own and that this same scapegoat mechanism, with all the self-deception it entails, is what cements our own bonds of solidarity and safeguards our self-esteem. If we do become convinced, however, that this insidious mechanism is at work in our own communities, then the pressing question becomes whether there's an alternative. Given how conflict-prone and resentful we tend to be, can our societies survive without the scapegoat mechanism and the pack mentality to hold them together?

Many people would pin their hopes on religion, but *True Blood* shows us how religions can sometimes be the worst perpetrators of scapegoating violence, especially when they teach that such violence is commanded by God. Girard even goes so far as to suggest that religion itself originally grew out of the scapegoating process. His theory is highly controversial among religious scholars, maybe even more so than the Vampire Rights Amendment is among human beings in the world *of True Blood*, but it's worth considering for its potential to shed light on the two religious cults that have figured most prominently in *True Blood* so far—Steve and Sarah Newlin's Fellowship of the Sun and Maryann Forrester's religion of the God Who Comes (or, as it so happens, *not*).

Girard imagines that at some point in the remote past human beings began to notice that escalating conflicts in the community would be quelled whenever people united to kill or expel a scapegoat. Afterward, everyone is relieved, having set aside their differences and channeled all of their hostility and resentment outside the community. Over time, the community learns to ritualize this process to gain the same result, first with ritual human sacrifice but later with an animal victim or even some inanimate object that bears symbolic significance. Girard believes that religion was born from such sacrificial rituals, which attempt to restore the peace and harmony originally experienced when the community came together in the fellowship of those who spill the scapegoat's blood or consign their victim's body to flames. In time, they may come to believe that their god demands these sacrifices as a way of dealing with sin or as a condition of receiving divine favor.[22]

Bound to Maryann's meat-upholstered tree as "zombie-eyed" Eggs approaches with a knife, Sam hears the crowd's bloodthirsty screams of "Sacrifice him!" But thanks to Bill Compton's clever scheme, the only person sacrificed that day is Maryann herself. Although it was certainly not Maryann's intention, her death seems to have accomplished the very purpose for which Girard believes ritual sacrifice was instituted—it puts an end to the escalating mayhem and allows everyone to return to some semblance of normal life (or at least as normal as life ever gets in Bon Temps). No doubt, similar cries of "Sacrifice him!" would have filled Godric's ears if the Newlins had been able to carry out their ritual of Meeting the Sun. From a Girardian perspective, this barbaric sacrament represents a return to the generative roots of all religion. Through it, the Newlins hoped to galvanize and solidify their congregation's commitment to their cause—which just happened to be launching an apocalyptic war between humans and vampires in which the latter would be annihilated. Thankfully, however, the sacrifice never occurs, with the result that the Newlins end up openly quarreling during a television interview, the debacle apparently having unleashed a bevy of bottled-up resentments of the sort that scapegoating is supposed to quash.

The most curious aspect of this whole affair is the disclosure that Godric had actually handed himself over the Newlins to be sacrificed as a kind of suicidal performance, much as Christians believe Jesus, whom Godric wishes he had met, allowed himself to be arrested and executed by his enemies.

Godric's motivation seems to have been a combination of guilt for his past crimes, a desire to spare some other vampire who might be sacrificed in his place ("They would have taken one of us sooner or later. I offered myself"), and, intriguingly, a belief that his sacrifice "might fix everything somehow."[23] Since Godric doesn't elaborate on this last motive, we can only speculate that he thought that his Christlike gesture of offering himself as a sacrifice might in some way atone not only for his own sins, but also for the murder of Steve's father and perhaps even help to reconcile the vampire and human communities. But however good Godric's intentions may have been, the expectation that any permanent peace can be brought about by sacrificial violence seems at best dangerously naive.

In the end, Godric stages his own ritual of meeting the sun atop the roof of the Dallas vampire nest, witnessed only by a tearful Sookie. Dressed in white, the traditional color of martyrdom, he queries this lone chaperone of his suicide about her religious beliefs. "Do you believe in God?" he asks. "Yes," she replies from the heart. But when Godric wants to know what sort of punishment she imagines awaits him for his centuries of crime, she answers with a few short syllables that underscore the immense distance that separates her God from the violent deity worshipped by those like the Newlins and Maryann. "God doesn't punish," she says, "God forgives." Implicit in that simple theological formula is a wager that forgiveness, rather than scapegoating violence, might be the best way to repair the damage done to our communities and our souls by the bad things that happen and the bad things we do.

That may sound incredible. But if a maenad can imagine herself into existence, who knows what else might be possible?

NOTES

1. Episode 212, "Beyond Here Lies Nothin'."
2. Ibid.
3. Ibid.

4. Friedrich Nietzsche, *Beyond Good and Evil*, aphorism 230, in *The Basic Writings of Nietzsche*, trans. Walter Kaufman (New York: Modern Library, 2000), p. 349.

5. Ibid., aphorism 68, p. 270.

6. Ibid., aphorism 156, p. 280.

7. "True Blood's Michelle Forbes Ponders 'The Riddle of Maryann,'" www.tvguide.com/news/true-blood-forbes-1007941.aspx.

8. *The Republic of Plato*, 2nd ed., trans. Allan Bloom (New York: Basic Books, 1991), p. 172 (492b–c).

9. Ibid., p. 172 (492c).

10. Ibid.

11. Thanks to Bruce McClelland for pointing out this connection.

12. *The Birth of Tragedy*, section 1, in *The Basic Writings of Nietzsche*, p. 36.

13. Episode 207, "Release Me."

14. Zigmunt Bauman, *Postmodern Ethics* (Cambridge, MA: Blackwell, 1993), p. 132.

15. Ibid.

16. René Girard, *Violence and the Sacred* (Baltimore: Johns Hopkins Univ. Press, 1979), p. 4.

17. Ibid., p. 2.

18. Episode 204, "Shake and Fingerpop."

19. We can get a good sense of this whole process with a quick image search on the Web for "lynching photos." These were once hot-selling items of the American pop culture. Typically they show African American corpses swinging from a tree or burning on a fire while a huge crowd of smiling white faces gathers around, proudly pointing to the "strange fruit." When *True Blood*'s theme song mentions doing "bad things with you," we should bear in mind that bad things like these are no more than a few decades in the past.

20. It's not only in fiction that vampires are scapegoats. In his *Slayers and Their Vampires: A Cultural History of Killing the Dead* (Ann Arbor: Univ. of Michigan Press, 2006), Bruce McClelland, who also wrote the chapter "Un-True Blood: The Politics of Artificiality" in this volume, describes how vampire folklore was first developed in the Balkans out of the need of communities for a scapegoat.

21. René Girard, *Evolution and Conversion: Dialogues on the Origins of Culture* (New York: Continuum, 2007), p. 262.

22. Girard presents his theory of religion in *Violence and the Sacred*. See also "The Victimage Mechanism as the Basis of Religion," chapter 1 in *Things Hidden Since the Foundation of the World* (Stanford, CA: Stanford Univ. Press, 1978), pp. 3–30. Girard, who is a Christian, notes that there are many passages in the Bible that appear to repudiate scapegoating and sacrificial religion, but he also acknowledges that historically Christianity has had a rather spotty record when it comes to living up to its professed ideals.

23. Episode 209, "I Will Rise Up."

ARE VAMPIRES UNNATURAL?

Andrew Terjesen and Jenny Terjesen

In an anti–Vampire Rights Amendment political ad (which can be found on disc 6 of the *True Blood* season 1 DVD set), one of the "men on the street" states, when asked about vampires, "They're so—so unnatural." This is not the only time in the *True Blood* series (or in the Southern Vampire Mysteries on which the series is based) that vampires are condemned because they're "unnatural." When Godric gets ready to meet the sun on a Dallas rooftop, he tells Eric: "Our existence is insanity."[1] The implication is that vampires should not exist because they are "unnatural." But before we stake Bill, Eric, Pam, and Jessica, it's important to consider what we're really saying when we call vampires "unnatural."

One common stereotype of the philosopher is someone who's overly obsessed with seemingly unnecessary distinctions that are often dismissed as "just semantics." And while there may be some truth to this stereotype, bear in mind that *semantics* is just another word for *meaning*. Obviously, the word *unnatural* doesn't mean the same thing as *immoral* or *impossible*. What we can forget—and what a philosopher might want to call to our attention—is that we sometimes use the word *unnatural* in a way that obscures how it differs in meaning from one or both of these other words. Before we can draw any conclusions from the fact that vampires are unnatural, we need to take a serious look at what that word could mean and examine the consequences of the different ways in which we might use it.

Viruses, Predation, and Evolution

When considering what "unnatural" might mean, we could start by looking at how nature is understood in the modern world within the science of evolutionary biology. From an evolutionary perspective, "natural" could refer to those properties of a creature that help it survive and reproduce. Moreover, since resources are limited, selective pressures that cause species to change are constantly being applied. Glamouring their prey may be a natural way for vampires to hunt humans right now, but over time people with a resistance to glamour would escape the vampires and could create a human species that has to be hunted in a different way. Then vampires might evolve to be sparkly or made of marble to better catch and kill their prey. Since species do change on an evolutionary scale, there is no reason to claim that some traits are definitively more natural than others. The most one could say is that some traits are currently more helpful to survival than others.

After the Great Revelation, vampires asserted that they really are people, albeit people who had been infected with a virus that makes them the way they are, with their "dead" physiology, their allergies to silver and sunlight, their blood thirst. It's this explanation that Sookie Stackhouse believes when she meets her first vampire, Bill Compton, and it's partly because of this explanation that she believes vampires should have equal rights and be treated fairly. Who can help getting a virus? Besides, the ability to live with this virus might be just another evolutionary step. Contracting and surviving a virus can lead to developing an immunity. Perhaps vampires have developed an immunity to death. Even if there's a downside (like a thirst for human blood), evolution might select for this condition if it's beneficial to the species overall.[2]

But maybe when people criticize vampires as unnatural, what they're really saying is that vampires don't play by the rules. Hypnotically attractive predators would seem to have an unfair advantage. Unfair, however, is not the same as unnatural. There are certainly predators in nature, including human hunters, who use color or scent or other means to attract prey. Notions of fairness aren't really part of the modern scientific conception of nature. Instead we may need to approach the issue in terms of the supernatural, which transcends our scientific categories. We'll address that later.

"A Purpose for Everything That God Creates"

If the imperative of nature is to survive, there's no reason to think that vampires are unnatural in an evolutionary sense. If anything, they are better competitors than us humans. However, people often use "unnatural" to refer to something that goes against the so-called natural order. In evolutionary theory, the natural order is not a very interesting concept. Species are constantly struggling to gain access to scarce resources, so any order that's produced will last only until some species develops a way to outcompete the others. There's no sense in modern evolutionary biology that nature ever has a way that it is *supposed* to be. But that wasn't always the case in science.

According to the ancient Greek philosopher Aristotle (384–322 B.C.E.), we don't truly understand something unless we understand the various causes that explain why that thing behaves as it does and how it came to be in the natural world. One of those causes that we need to understand is the "final cause," the reason or purpose for which something exists. The final cause explains a thing's natural course of development. An acorn has the final cause of becoming an oak tree, and so the way it grows is explained by what it is "trying" to become. The final cause also explains the design of each thing. Trees have roots for the sake of maintaining their existence as trees, whereas a tiger has claws and teeth in order to maintain its tiger nature, and so on. Everything in the universe, from pebbles on a beach to stars in the sky, has a final cause, reflecting what the thing is naturally equipped to do and can therefore do better than anything else. Aristotle says that the final cause of human beings is to engage in a life of reason. And the final cause of a platypus—well, let's just say that it was a good thing for his theory that Aristotle never visited Australia.

As Sookie wrestles with her attraction to Bill, trying to figure out whether it's right or proper, Gran advises her, "I just think there is a purpose for everything that God creates, whether it's a unique ability or a cup of overpriced coffee with too much milk . . . or a vampire. God will reveal that purpose when the time is right."[3] Gran's remark highlights a difference between Aristotle's idea of a final cause and the way in which later interpreters understood the concept.[4] Aristotle's final cause was simply about *intrinsic finality*, meaning that the purpose of a thing was always considered with reference to the individual nature of the creature, the fulfillment of its own inherent potential. What Gran is invoking is *extrinsic finality*, which is the purpose something serves with regard to other creatures and the universe as a whole.

The Christian philosopher Thomas Aquinas (1225–1274), who's often described as "baptizing" Aristotle in the Middle Ages, understands the final cause as both an *intrinsic finality* and an *extrinsic finality* determined by God. As Aquinas put it, "God in his wisdom is the creator of all things and is related to them in the same way as an artist is related to his works of art. . . . He governs all the actions and motions that are found in individual creatures."[5] *Extrinsic finality* requires a belief in a being that has a plan for the entire universe and orders the intrinsic final causes of individual beings in order to realize that plan. For Gran and Aquinas, this being is the Christian God who designed human beings to discover the truths of the universe. Since final causes are defined by some divine plan, when we call something "unnatural," we are effectively saying that it goes against the plan. And since the plan was created by the supreme superrational being, it's a bad thing to go against the plan.

It's important to respect Gran's hesitation to specify the extrinsic final cause of vampires—after all, who can know the mind of the divine?—but let's try to consider what it *might* be. Aquinas's final cause is supposed to help define what a creature is by appealing to the function it serves in the universe. It seems that what vampires do best is prey on other creatures, specifically human beings. As the vampire bartender Longshadow puts it, "That's what we are . . . death."[6] It would seem to follow that the purpose of vampires is to be the ultimate predator. We might not like the fact that their prey is usually human beings, but that doesn't mean it's unnatural. As Gran says, God must have had a reason for creating such predators.

Like Lions Who Want to Caress Antelopes

In *Dead to the World*, the fourth book of the Southern Vampire Mysteries, Sookie has to update an amnesiac Eric Northman. She describes how she rescued Bill and how Eric healed her after she'd been staked, giving her blood for strength so that she might accomplish her mission. And she confesses to having killed the "vampire ho Lorena" in self-defense during the rescue. Eric asks her if she'd ever killed anyone before that. Sookie says, "No, I'm a *human*. I don't have to kill anyone to live," which leads to a discussion of murder and how people often kill each other for reasons that have nothing to do with a need to eat or drink blood.[7] Since human beings can survive without killing one another for blood, it's not natural for them to prey on one another. Eric claims that all vampires are murderers, but Sookie counters him with an analogy to another natural predator who has to kill to survive:

> "But in a way, you're like lions,"
>> Eric looked astonished. "Lions?" he said weakly.
>> "Lions all kill stuff." At the moment, this idea seemed like an inspiration.
>> "So you're predators, like lions and raptors. But you use what you kill. You have to kill to eat."[8]

Comparing vampires to a predator like a lion isn't all that far-fetched. They both possess great speed and strength. And they both have to eat a certain kind of diet in order to survive. Eric sees a flaw in Sookie's analogy, though. As he responds:

> "The catch in that comforting theory being that we look almost exactly like you. And we used to be you. And we can love you, as well as feed off you. You could hardly say the lion wanted to caress the antelope."
>> Suddenly there was something in the air that hadn't been there the moment before. I felt a little like an antelope that was being stalked—by a lion that was a deviant.[9]

Vampires have very good camouflage as predators. The secrecy in which they enshroud themselves is another of their advantages. They keep the locations of their resting places hidden. It is clear in both the *True Blood* series and the Southern Vampire Mysteries that vampires are secretive about their abilities and their weaknesses. Even after announcing their existence to humans, vampires try to keep their vulnerability to silver, the healing powers of their blood, and many other facts about themselves under wraps. It's never quite clear what is myth and what is truth when dealing with vampires, although Sookie gets a behind-the-scenes look that's not permitted to many human beings. So they're not only predators; they're an exclusive, secret society of predators. One might be tempted to call this unnatural, because animals are not usually so secretive—lions don't infiltrate gazelle society in order to convince gazelles that lions are a myth. However, just because something doesn't occur in nature (yet) does not make it automatically unnatural. Besides, many animals use camouflage, lures, playing dead, and so on, to hunt or to escape predators. So simple deception isn't unusual or unnatural at all. From the perspective of final causes, something has to go against the way things were designed in order to be unnatural.

The exchange between Sookie and Eric suggests that vampires have violated the normal way of preying upon creatures. The fact that vampires go about their predation in "strange" ways, such as sleeping with (and in some cases, loving) their food, might seem unnatural. It also might seem unfair that vampires use all sorts of tricks to lure their prey. However, to move from strange or unfair to unnatural is possible from the perspective of Thomas Aquinas only if you know what the actual purposes of things are. Otherwise, you're just guessing as to what is the right or wrong way for a given creature to survive. As the representative of the American Vampire League, Nan Flanagan, points out to a human interviewer in a segment on *In Focus: Vampires in America*, "I'm not interested in labels. Who's to say what's natural? Who's to say that what my body can do is any less natural than what your body can do?"[10]

The Problem with Purpose

Unfortunately, it's very difficult to know for sure if you have deduced the extrinsic final cause of a particular animal. Very early on in *True Blood*, Malcolm, a vampire acquaintance of

Bill's, asks, "If we can't kill people, what's the point of being a vampire?"[11] More disturbingly, vampires tend to see the purpose of humans as being similar to the purpose most people would give for cattle.[12] As Lorena tells Bill when he tries to race off to save Sookie from the Fellowship of the Sun: "You are vampire. They are food. That's your nature."[13]

The magister at Bill's trial for killing Longshadow has absolutely no patience for Bill's defense that he was protecting Sookie. "Humans exist to serve us," he says. "That is their only value."[14] Based on what we've seen, these views are shared by the majority of vampires, and only the rare vampire like Bill seems to think that living off TruBlood is not a violation of the purpose of vampire existence.

The attitudes that these vampires express make the perspective of Steve Newlin of the Fellowship of the Sun sound a little less intolerant and a little more realistic. "Have you found that they want to kill us all, dominate us with their foul ways and empty promises?" he asks Sookie and Hugo as they attempt to infiltrate the Fellowship's headquarters in *Living Dead in Dallas*, the second book of the Southern Vampire Mysteries.[15] Newlin and his Fellowship are fond of talking about how all vampires are damned, how they're outside of God's plan, and how God has a special place in hell for vampires once they're staked or burned. But he doesn't present too many arguments to help us understand why these things are so or how he knows them.

We can only guess what kind of theology, if any, vampires have; but it's clear that the vampire belief about the purpose of human beings conflicts with Reverend Newlin's belief that humans exist on this earth to glorify God. This particular disagreement reveals the major problem with trying to use final causes to understand nature—we can't tell what something's purpose is by looking at it. The only way to really know the purpose of something (at least in the sense of extrinsic final cause) would be to know the intent of its creator (assuming there is one). In the context of morality or religion, such speculation seems permissible. However, within the perspective of modern science, purposes aren't anything that can be observed or measured and so have no place in our study of nature.

Aristotle's notion of science as including the study of final causes inhibited the development of modern science for a number of centuries. The tendency to look for purpose in things can lead us to think we have figured something out because we think we know what its purpose should be. A classic example is in the study of optics in the medieval period. Medieval scientists thought that white light had to be pure because it was the light of God, so that colors were the result of matter corrupting pure spiritual light. This theory fit very well with their ideas about the purpose of things in the universe. But it also caused medieval optics to resist the idea that colors were the basic forms of light and that white light was the result of combining all of the colors into one. Until theology was removed from optics, progress in understanding things such as prisms and how to manipulate the light spectrum was hindered. And don't even get us started on the idea that diseases like the bubonic plague were punishments from God for sinful behaviors as opposed to the results of poor pest management.

The fact that final causes often led to bad science caused philosophers in the seventeenth century to banish final causes from the study of nature. The philosopher René Descartes (1596–1650) was one of the main early proponents of turning physics into the study of matter in motion without any reference to purposes, either intrinsic or extrinsic. Descartes' argument was based in part on showing how mechanistic explanations were often better than explanations that relied on final causes. After all, it makes more sense to try to describe a vampire's need for blood in terms of a parasite like a leech than to come up with some explanation as to why human-size bloodsuckers must exist. But the crux of Descartes' argument was how absurd it was to think of everything in the universe as trying to fulfill its purpose. As he noted in the "Sixth Replies" to his *Meditations on First Philosophy*, according to Aristotelian science, a rock falls to the earth because it is trying to reunite with the matter it resembles as opposed to fire, which rises to try and rejoin the fiery ether in the heavens.[16] But "trying" implies intentional effort, and it seems absurd to say that natural objects like rocks have mental states. It makes much more sense to talk about the movement of rocks in terms of the physical force of gravity.

The argument for making final causes a part of science in Aristotle was that we cannot make sense of the universe without invoking the purpose of all of the changes we observe. But that's only because Aristotle thought that their purpose explained how things came to be and took on the forms that they have. Vampires have fangs so that they can bite people, and unless they were *designed* to bite people, their being so well suited to sucking blood would seem an incredible coincidence. Aristotle's argument is based on the assumption that it's impossible for creatures to develop mechanisms so well suited for their survival by chance. But Aristotle wasn't aware of modern evolutionary theory, which explains how chance *can* produce something that works very well *for the moment*. To fall back on the idea of design means that we're no longer trying to figure out how something might have evolved by natural processes—and if we abandon that effort, we hinder science. For a long time, it was thought that the evolution of the eye could not be explained. But now we have some interesting and plausible theories that would never have been put forward if scientists had thrown up their hands and said that the eye is so complex that it must be a product of intelligent design.

Bear in mind that taking final causes out of science is not the same as removing them from existence altogether. Evolutionary theory doesn't have to be incompatible with a religious perspective that concerns itself with things that go beyond what can be learned through the study of nature. However, our knowledge of *natural* processes is derived from science. If final causes are not a part of the natural processes that science investigates, then it makes no sense to say that something is *unnatural* because it violates some theory about its purpose. One could make a moral argument against acting a certain way, but that's very different from saying that vampires are "unnatural."

Supes Aren't Natural— They're *Super*-Natural!

Vampires are clearly unnatural if you use *natural* as the opposite of *supernatural*. In that case, being supernatural makes them by definition *unnatural*. As the Johnson University professor Robert Hill points out in the faux documentary *In Focus: Vampires in America*, the virus theory of vampirism isn't an adequate explanation of the physiology of vampires. It is unusual for a virus to act like a steroid and reanimate dead tissue. Plus, it's not clear why a virus would make someone vulnerable to silver or unable to enter a private residence without an invitation. The interviewer eventually says to Dr. Hill, "What's your explanation for this? It sounds positively supernatural." And Dr. Hill admits that it may just be a supernatural phenomenon.

The word *supernatural*, as used by the interviewer and by Dr. Hill, seems to refer to something that can't be explained by the laws of physics. Further evidence for the supernatural character of vampires can be found in Bill's explanation to Jessica Hamby of the process of "making" a vampire. The method for turning a human being into a vampire is a closely guarded secret among vampires, but it seems that the requirements are that the maker drains the victim until they are almost dead and then has the victim drink some of the maker's blood. But that's still not enough, as the victim needs to be buried in the earth with his maker before the process can be completed. As Bill explains the process to Jessica, "Then I shared my 'essence' with you . . . it's part of the process. It's magical. Even we don't fully understand how it works."[17] There seems to be no reason that sleeping together in the earth should cause such a transformation.[18] After all, viruses don't care about their hosts' sleeping arrangements.

The epitome of the supernatural is magic, and the world of Sookie Stackhouse abounds with magical creatures, including shifters, Weres, fairies, demons, maenads, and who knows what else. Everything that defies our current understanding of physics seems to have a magical explanation, including Sookie's mind-reading abilities.[19] In describing the nature of the maenad Maryann Forrester, the queen of Louisiana makes it clear that Maryann's magical nature is outside of the realm of physics. As she puts it, "Never underestimate the power of blind faith. It can manifest in ways that bend the laws of physics or break them entirely."[20] Maryann lived about four thousand years because she believed she could, and she died because she doubted her immortality for a moment. When we talk about "losing the will to live," it's a metaphorical description of how someone might stop trying to survive. Only in a magical realm could the will to survive stave off natural processes of decay and the usual effects of bullets and other weapons.

On the other hand, just as we should be careful about ascribing purposes to things, we should be equally wary of assuming that we completely understand the laws of physics. An exchange between Sookie and Bill in an early episode of *True Blood* highlights this fact:

> Bill: I have no heartbeat. I have no need to breathe. There are no electrical impulses in my body. What animates you does not animate me.
>
> Sookie: What does animate you, then? Blood?

Bill: Magic.

Sookie: Come on, Bill. I may look naive, but I'm not. You need to remember that.

Bill: You think that it's not magic that keeps you alive? Just 'cause you understand the mechanics of how something works doesn't make it less of a miracle, which is just another word for "magic." We're all kept alive by magic, Sookie. My magic's just a little different from yours.[21]

Just because science can't explain how something works, that doesn't mean that it works unnaturally. What we call magic now might simply be natural processes we haven't yet figured out. A number of unexplained phenomena in contemporary physics resemble magic—such as the way that a particle in one part of the world can affect the state of a particle in another part of the world without anything we can observe linking the two. Likewise, a lot of things about vampires, werewolves, witches, and other supes do not fit our current worldview. But that doesn't mean we won't someday understand how a virus can makes us almost immortal.

On the other hand, it might be a mistake to insist that vampires must have a natural explanation. Either way, it shouldn't be a factor in determining whether vampires should be allowed to exist alongside humans. When facing the possibility that Bill really is undead and that he's animated by supernatural rather than natural forces, Sookie has a much harder time accepting him as boyfriend material. She does come around, though. Her hesitation is understandable, but in the end she presumably realized that something shouldn't be rejected just because it's supernatural. After all, angels and fairies are supernatural creatures, but people don't usually advocate for their destruction. What really concerns people about supes like vampires, shifters, and Weres isn't the lack of a scientific explanation for their existence. It's the fear that they'll use their abilities to hurt people.

Unnatural Is Not Automatically Wrong

Before Godric commits suicide, he declares, "Our existence is insanity. We don't belong here."[22] His assumption seems to be that vampires are unnatural and that their existence must therefore also be immoral. But that doesn't really hold water. First, we haven't yet established that vampires are truly unnatural. Second, being unnatural isn't the same as being immoral, and it's immorality that is really the issue with vampires. In the Southern Vampire Mysteries, the ancient vampire who decides to meet the sun is Godfrey, and he bears a passing resemblance to Godric of *True Blood*. But Godfrey wants to meet the sun not just because he considers the existence of vampires in general to be an abomination, but also because he considers his *own* existence to be monstrous.

> "But we take the blood of innocents." Godfrey's blue pale eyes fixed on mine.
>
> "Who is innocent?" I asked rhetorically, hoping I didn't sound too much like Pontius Pilate asking, "what is the truth?" when he knew damn well.
>
> "Well, children," Godfrey said.
>
> "Oh, you . . . fed on children?" I put my hand over my mouth.
>
> [. . .] He was suffering, and I was truly sorry for that. But if he'd been human, I'd have said he deserved the electric chair without thinking twice.[23]

There are, of course, human monsters who prey on children. Godfrey isn't human, but he once was, so his predation still seems pretty horrifying. The issue here isn't so much the unnaturalness of preying upon children, however; it's the immorality of the practice. Even with Godric's suicide in *True Blood*, the issue isn't really about the naturalness of vampiric existence, but about the morality of what vampires do. As Godric prepares to greet the sun, he has the following exchange with Eric, whom he sired in the television series (although not in the books):

> Godric: We don't belong here. It's not right. We're not right.
>
> Eric: You taught me there is no right or wrong. Only survival or death.
>
> Godric: I told a lie.[24]

The issue is right and wrong, not a question of nature but a question of choice.

Moral philosophers have long recognized that we can't look to the way things are to determine the way they ought to be. This mistaken bit of reasoning has become known as the "Is-Ought Fallacy." If we were to rely on nature to define our moral sensibilities, then anything that furthers our survival would be morally permissible. There would be, as Eric puts it, "no right or wrong. Only survival or death." Few think that morality should be based on pure unadulterated self-interest, and there are very good arguments as to why morality should be about more than just what keeps us alive. Our current understanding of the human brain suggests that we have a tendency to think in terms of in-groups and out-groups, which tends to foster racism and other forms of discrimination, but that doesn't make racism okay. An understanding of the working of nature cannot tell how we *ought* to live. At best it can tell us what might help us achieve our goals, but it can't tell us what goals would be moral for us to pursue. By the same token, just because something lacks a natural explanation, that doesn't automatically make it immoral.

The only way we could equate "unnatural" and "immoral" is within a framework like Thomas Aquinas's, where we have certain ideas about the way the universe is *supposed* to work. But we've seen that we don't have any scientific evidence for the real purpose of things in the universe. Instead of trying to import divine purposes into science and treating them as uncontested facts, maybe we should treat ideas about extrinsic final causes as moral frameworks that we need to argue for or against in the same way that we debate other controversial moral ideas in our society.

Perhaps in the end the fear is not so much that vampires are unnatural but that they're so constituted by nature that it's impossible for them to choose to do the right thing, as though they really were spawn of Satan. Sookie, in describing her fears about Bill, touches upon the idea that vampires might be inherently immoral creatures when she says, "He doesn't think like we do. He doesn't feel the way we do—if he feels at all."[25] It may be that the nature of vampires causes them to have a concept of morality different from our own. Certainly, Bill sees no problem with disposing of the uncle who molested Sookie. But it's not clear that what Bill did was inherently immoral or any different from what many human beings might have done. Bill's abilities make it easier to escape detection, but one could argue that he delivered a just punishment. Regardless of whether we think Bill acted rightly in this instance, it's still not his nature as a vampire that we're judging, but his choices as a moral being.

The fact that vampires like Bill and Eddie Gauthier are trying to mainstream is proof that it's possible for vampires to choose to live a moral life. It may be harder for them, but it's also hard for people with addictions or mental illness. We wouldn't say that addicts must die because it's difficult for them to choose to do the right thing, and we shouldn't make such a claim about vampires who are trying to live a moral life, either. We need to take them on a case-by-case basis and not simply judge them based on the "nature" of their species.

NOTES

1. Episode 209, "I Will Rise Up."

2. Of course, the fact that vampires are sterile greatly complicates this explanation, since evolution works by selecting traits that can be passed on to offspring. If vampirism is a disease, the "making" of a vampire reproduces the genetic material of the virus but not the host. As a result, vampires might not really be an independent species, and this is one more reason we can't apply the biological concept of "natural" to them.

3. Episode 103, "Mine."

4. Although our essay has benefited in many ways from the work of our editors, we'd like to especially thank George Dunn for his comments on this topic, which led us to be more precise about the notion of final cause and gave us a vocabulary with which to articulate the differences.

5. Thomas Aquinas, *On Politics and Ethics* (*Summa Theologica*, I–II, question 93, article 1), trans. Paul Sigmund (New York: W.W. Norton, 1988), p.48.

6. Episode 104, "Escape from Dragon House."

7. Charlaine Harris, *Dead to the World* (New York: Ace Books, 2004), p. 53.

8. Ibid.

9. Ibid.

10. Included as a special feature on disc 6 of the *True Blood* season 1 DVD.

11. Episode 102, "The First Taste."

12. For more on human beings as cattle in the eyes of vampires, see Ariadne Blayde and George A. Dunn's chapter in this volume, "Pets, Cattle, and Higher Life Forms on *True Blood*."

13. Episode 207, "Release Me."

14. Episode 110, "I Don't Wanna Know."

15. Charlaine Harris, *Living Dead in Dallas* (New York: Ace Books, 2002), p. 131.

16. René Descartes, *Meditations, Objections and Replies*, trans. Roger Ariew and Donald Cress (Indianapolis: Hackett Publishing, 2006), p. 178.

17. Episode 111, "To Love Is to Bury."

18. To be fair, this explanation of making is unique to the series *True Blood*. In Charlaine Harris's *Definitely Dead* (New York: Ace Books, 2006), a new vampire rises after sitting in stasis in a closet, and his maker was already dead, so no sharing of essence or burial in the earth was required.

19. At least in the books, where Sookie's magical, fairy heritage seems to be the likely explanation for her abilities (she reads minds and is immune to glamouring) as well as why her telepathy doesn't really work on other "supes."

20. Episode 211, "Frenzy."

21. Episode 103, "Mine."

22. Episode 209, "I Will Rise Up."

23. Charlaine Harris, *Living Dead in Dallas*, p. 155.

24. Episode 209, "I Will Rise Up."

25. Episode 105, "Sparks Fly Out."

DOES GOD HATE FANGS?

Adam Barkman

During the opening credits for *True Blood*, a sign reading "God hates fangs" briefly flashes across the screen. This sign represents only one response to vampires in the series, but it does raise a couple of interesting and ancient questions: Are there beings that are inherently evil, beings whose very existence constitutes an offense to the God whom the major religious traditions of the West regard as perfectly good? And if so, how could that be, given that God is also said to be the all-powerful creator of all that exists, which would include vampires, if there are any?

From these questions we get a couple of related ones: Are all vampires evil? And if so, were they created that way? Let's look at how these questions were dealt with by some notable theologians in the past and then consider what *True Blood* might have to say on this subject today.

Doing Bad Things with Good Gifts

It wasn't until the seventeenth century that anyone in Christendom produced a systematic study of vampires. So when the Catholic theologian Leo Allatius (1586–1669) included a discussion of vampires in his treatise *On Certain Modern Opinions among the Greeks* (*De Graecorum Hodie Quirundam Opinationibus*, 1645), the subject of vampires became a matter seriously discussed by Western theologians for the first time. Writing at the height of the European witch craze, during which thousands of accused witches were put on trial, tortured, and executed for having consorted with Satan and his demons, Allatius argues that Greek vampires could be real creatures made possible by the work of demons or the arch-demon Satan. Allatius seems to have been unaware of the virus theory propagated by the vampires in Charlaine Harris's Southern Vampire Mysteries, according to which vampires are human beings infected with a virus that, among other things, makes them appear dead for a few days and leaves them allergic to sunlight, silver, and garlic.[1] He was, however, aware of the infamous *Hammer of Witches* (*Malleus Maleficarum*), written in 1486 by Heinrich Kramer and Jacob Sprenger, two leaders of the Inquisition in Germany.[2] The *Hammer of Witches*, which supplied Allatius with some of his arguments, was written to refute the claim that witchcraft doesn't exist, to spell out the dangerous powers of witches, and to describe how to prosecute them. There's probably a copy somewhere in Steve Newlin's library. This handbook for witch hunters and inquisitors was itself heavily undergirded by theological arguments from the great medieval theologian and philosopher Thomas Aquinas (1225–1274).

Like many medieval Christians, Aquinas believed that evil demons really exist and can exert a sinister influence on human affairs. But how could these creatures bent on evil exist if everything was created by a perfectly good and all-powerful God? Aquinas's answer was simple: free will. Aquinas shared the belief of many Christian theologians that evil was, strictly speaking, nothing or no-*thing*. According to this view, evil isn't something that can really be said to exist *inherently* in something, like fangs in a vampire's mouth or lust in Jason Stackhouse's loins. These things, like everything else that exists, were created good and retain their goodness for as long as they're used in proper ways. God doesn't hate fangs or sex or even the silver chains that the Rattrays used to bind Bill Compton in order to drain his blood. But neither does God approve of all the ways these things are used. So why then doesn't God prevent their improper use? Why does God let people "do bad things"?

God created everything good, and one of those good things is the free will given to selected creatures—angels, human beings, and possibly others who weren't on Aquinas's radar screen, such as vampires, shapeshifters, weres, fairies, and maenads. Free will permits human beings (and similarly endowed creatures) to choose between good and evil; that is, between honoring God by treating others right or doing just the opposite. Unfortunately, many of us make the wrong choices.

Aquinas believed that among the creatures who made bad use of God's gift of free will were some of the angels. Because they honored themselves more than they honored God, they fell from grace and became the evil angels or demons. Demons differ from the good angels in saying to God "my will, not thine," instead of "not my will, but thine," as they should be saying. In rebellion against God, they also seek to ruin the lives of human beings. Lettie Mae Thornton, whose belief in the traditional Christian teaching about the reality of demons leaves her vulnerable to Miss Jeanette's con job, may well believe that it was one of these rebellious angels that possessed her and caused her addiction to alcohol.[3] But Aquinas emphasized that God didn't create these demons to be evil, any more than God created Miss Jeanette to be a con artist. To the contrary, God created them good and even endowed them with one of the greatest of all goods, free will. Their evil results from misusing God's good gift.

"Through the Virtue of Demons"

Aquinas never got around to addressing the topic of vampires, who in any case wouldn't become well known in Catholic Christendom until several centuries later, but he did have some interesting things to say about witches that would influence Allatius's later writings on vampires. Granting that demons may exist and that they may have human followers that include witches, do witches and their kind have any real power? Aquinas believed witchcraft was indeed a real power but that it required three key components in order to work: a demon, a witch, and the permission of God.[4]

Even after being rejected by the demons, God continues to respect their free will. Just as God didn't prevent Rene Lenier from killing Adele Stackhouse, God sometimes permits demons to do what they want. Unfortunately for the rest of us, that means that demonic powers can disrupt our world, often in the form of diseases, storms, and other calamities that Aquinas believed were sometimes, though not always, the work of demons. More relevant to *True Blood*, demons can also enter into contracts with human beings who have misused their free will and rejected God. People can thus acquire powers "through the virtue of demons" that surpass the powers of normal human beings.[5]

Aquinas might have proposed human-demonic complicity as an explanation of how Maryann Forrester the maenad acquired her extraordinary powers and longevity. According to the vampire queen Sophie-Anne of Louisiana, Maryann started out human, perhaps as "a wild young girl who's married to some jerk who treats you like property," and was drawn to the worship of Dionysus, a "religion that encourages you to get hammered, run naked through the woods, have sex with whoever, whatever, and it's all part of getting closer to God."[6] Since many of the early church fathers regarded the pagan gods as demons, it's very likely that Aquinas would have heard in Sophie-Anne's remarks about Maryann confirmation that the maenad's god was really one of those demons, if not actually Satan himself. Maryann's disciple, the shapeshifter Daphne, certainly doesn't shy away from that equation. "Dionysus, Satan," she rhapsodizes. "It's really just a kind of energy. Wild energy, like lust, anger, excess, violence. Basically all the fun stuff."[7] Fun stuff—like human sacrifice and cannibalism! Aquinas would have no hesitation in declaring this fun stuff to be the work of demons.

Allatius believed that vampires were possible in much the same way that Aquinas believed witches were. Remember that for Aquinas all that was required for witchcraft was a demon, a witch, and the permission of God. The same holds for vampires, according to Allatius, except that a dead body takes the place of the witch. The result is an animated but soulless corpse, controlled by and possessing demonic power. The demon-controlled vampire is associated with many of the same things the *Hammer of Witches* associates with the demon-controlled witch, a few of which are:

- A perverse sexual appetite, which is undoubtedly how an old-fashioned guy like Allatius would describe the appetites of *True Blood* vampires who get a sexual charge from biting their victims
- Sterility, infertility, and even child murder (think of Godfrey, from *Living Dead in Dallas*, the second book of the Southern Vampire Mysteries), for if God is associated with life, those who oppose God must be associated with barrenness and death
- Shapeshifting, something *True Blood* vampires don't do, having left that to the shapeshifters and the Weres
- The need to be invited in, for just as a witch must invite the demon to possess her, the vampire must be invited before entering a person's home
- Darkness and night, for if one of the most potent metaphors for God is light (just ask the Fellowship), it makes sense to associate darkness with those who hate God
- Bloodlust—or, we might even say, True Bloodlust

Being strongly linked to demons, vampires also shared their strengths and weaknesses, in particular, their powerful aversion to everything associated with the Christian God— images of the cross, holy water, Eucharistic wafers, and so on. As with demons, the vampire's chief foe was the Catholic priest, the true priest of the true God. Non-Christian religious symbols were useless against vampires, although "baptized" pre-Christian things, such as silver and garlic, were thought to be effective deterrents, silver because it cost Judas his life and garlic because of its well-known curative, and hence life-giving, properties.[8] Interestingly, the vampires of *True Blood*, despite being immune to the power of Christian symbols, still retain the traditional vampiric allergies to silver and garlic.

"We Vampires Aren't Minions of the Devil"

The last century has seen an enormous outpouring of vampire literature, much of it influenced to various degrees by secularism and religious pluralism. Vampires have been depicted as space aliens, the product of scientific experiments, highly evolved humans, and any number of other things that amount to a rejection of the medieval Christian view that vampires are corpses animated by demons. The questions surrounding God, evil, and vampires have also changed, and one of the best examples of this is the HBO series *True Blood*, based on Charlaine Harris's Southern Vampire Mysteries.

The events of *True Blood* take place only a few years after vampires have first "come out of the coffin" and begun campaigning for equal rights with human beings. The human protagonists of the show aren't heroic vampire slayers fighting to rid the world of nocturnal bloodsuckers but mostly open-minded people who view vampires as rational creatures worthy of the same rights as human beings. That's a far cry from the era when vampires were lumped with demons and thought to be so far beyond the grace of God that they were to be neither tolerated nor treated with patient respect, but simply exorcized and exterminated.

What has changed? *True Blood* vampires are associated with neither demons nor obvious demonic power. They've become a unique race of beings, not simply instruments through which demons press their ongoing rebellion against God and everything good and right. "We vampires aren't minions of the Devil," explains Bill Compton. "We can stand before a cross or a Bible or in a church."[9] Bill proves this assertion by doing the very thing that Christians like Allatius would have deemed impossible, standing before a cross in church while addressing a meeting of the Descendants of the Glorious Dead. For the most part, only the Fellowship of the Sun, which Harris has called a Christian "hate group . . . based on fear and misunderstanding," would agree with Allatius's view of the vampire as a soulless demon-possessed corpse.[10] But the Fellowship's belief that these "creatures of the darkness [vampires] are undoubtedly the children of Satan" flies in the face of all of the evidence we see on the show that, like human beings, vampires have the freedom to choose to do good, even if, just like human beings, they don't always exercise it well.[11]

Vampires may no longer be associated with demons, but that's not to say that Christianity and its philosophical questions don't factor in to *True Blood*. Charlaine Harris is an active Episcopalian, and it's not hard to see how her own beliefs have influenced her writing of the Southern Vampire Mysteries and, through that source material, the show *True Blood*. For example, Harris says that one of the reasons she's an Episcopalian is that it's "an inclusive church," one that welcomes all people, including those whom other churches have excluded in the past, such as gays and lesbians.[12] Sookie Stackhouse and her grandmother are Methodists, but their attitude toward vampires reflects the same inclusivitism that Harris admires in her own Episcopal Church. Sookie tells her Gran, "I don't think Jesus would mind if someone was a vampire."[13] Gran completely agrees, presumably because she believes that vampires, no less than human beings, were created by God and not by rebellious demons squatting inside human corpses. "There is a purpose to everything God makes," she says, "even a vampire."[14]

The inherent goodness of vampires as vampires explains why explicitly Christian symbols are useless against them, as we learn when Sookie quizzes Bill on some of the vampire's rumored vulnerabilities.

> Sookie: Holy water?
> Bill: It's just water.
> Sookie: Crucifixes?
> Bill: Geometry.[15]

Harris says that Christian symbols don't work on vampires because "a symbol can only be effective against someone who believes in its power."[16] Her point is that there's no uniquely holy power in any material object—presumably not even the Eucharist (contrary to the position of the Episcopal Church)—such that they would repel creatures that have utterly rejected Christ. According to this view, Christian symbols are ineffective against vampires not because the Christian God doesn't exist (as Anne Rice argued in her early vampire novels), but because God just isn't all that concerned about endowing symbols with special holy power.

If vampires, just like angels and human beings, were created by God to fulfill a good purpose, then the only way they can become evil is in the same way that angels and human beings can—by misusing their free will. But there's no reason that a vampire who makes proper use of his or her free will can't be as morally upstanding as any human being. Bill, for instance, is a pretty good guy, not without his faults but certainly superior in many respects to morally reprobate human characters like the Rattrays, Sookie's uncle Bartlett, and Rene Lenier. Moreover, there doesn't seem to be any reason that a vampire, who's perfectly capable of entering a church and standing before a cross, couldn't actually become a *Christian*, although none of the vampires on *True Blood* actually are. The closest we come is Bill, who says he *"was* a Christian."[17]

Maybe he would consider becoming one again if there were fewer Christians like the members of the Fellowship of the Sun.

NOTES

1. Charlaine Harris, *Dead until Dark* (New York: Ace Books, 2001), p. 2.

2. Heinrich Kramer and Jacob Sprenger, *The Hammer of Witches: A Complete Translation of the Malleus Maleficarum*, trans. Christopher S. Mackay (Cambridge: Cambridge Univ. Press, 2009).

3. Of course, the alcoholic's blaming her addiction on a demon is an old story. Lettie Mae's story is unique in that her belief in demons seems to have actually contributed to her recovery rather than just serving as an excuse to stay drunk.

4. Thomas Aquinas, *Summa Theologica*, vol. 5, trans. Fathers of the English Dominican Province (Allen, TX: Christian Classics), 1981, pp. 2767–2768 (Suppl., Q. 58, Art. 2).

5. Kramer and Sprenger, *Hammer of Witches*, p. 92.

6. Episode 211, "Frenzy."

7. Episode 207, "Release Me."

8. Matthew 27:5.

9. Episode 105, "Sparks Fly Out"

10. Charlaine Harris, e-mail message to the author, October 25, 2009.

11. Episode 201, "Nothing but the Blood."

12. Charlaine Harris, e-mail message to the author, October 25, 2009. In 1994 the General Convention of the Episcopal Church passed a resolution stating that no one would be denied membership based solely on "marital status, sex, or sexual orientation." In 2009 the Council of Bishops officially opened ordination to all levels of the ministry to gays and lesbians, although the first openly gay bishop, Gene Robinson, had already been elected to his office six years earlier, in 2003. Not all members of the Episcopal Church have supported these moves, however, and many Episcopalians have left their church because of this controversy.

13. Episode 102, "The First Taste."

14. Episode 103, "Mine."

15. Episode 107, "Burning House of Love."

16. Charlaine Harris, e-mail message to the author, October 25, 2009.

17. Episode 110, "I Don't Wanna Know."

PART FIVE

"OUR EXISTENCE IS INSANITY": THE METAPHYSICS OF SUPERNATURAL BEINGS

A VAMPIRE'S HEART HAS ITS REASONS THAT SCIENTIFIC NATURALISM CAN'T UNDERSTAND

Susan Peppers-Bates and Joshua Rust

From *True Blood* to *Twilight*, vampires are hot. What explains the recent surge of popularity in vampire fiction, TV shows, and film? The vampire allures not simply because of the danger or taboo it presents, but also because of a romantic longing to return to an enchanted world that is apparently lost in the humdrum of the ordinary—a life ruled by science and not by religion, mysticism, or the mysterious. In Charlaine Harris's Southern Vampire Mysteries and *True Blood*, the HBO series based on the books, vampires, werewolves, shapeshifters, fairies, and other magical creatures populate the world. Sookie Stackhouse is initially attracted to the vampire Bill Compton because of how he differs from human beings. In particular, she appreciates Bill's resistance to her telepathic gifts, allowing her to enjoy silence after a lifetime of being unwillingly bombarded by other people's thoughts. That vampires differ from human beings is also a source of concern to Sookie, however.

Disenchanted Vampires

In a 1918 lecture at Munich University, the sociologist Max Weber (1864–1920) declared that "the fate of our times is characterized by rationalization and intellectualization and, above all, by the 'disenchantment of the world.'"[1] There are many ways to characterize the transition from an enchanted, premodern outlook to our contemporary worldview. We could describe it as the movement from superstition to justified belief. Or maybe as a shift from ascribing a personality to natural beings and forces, as when people might talk of willful trees and treasonous winds, to a more impersonal view of nature.[2] We might also describe the transition to the modern worldview as a reduction of the ways we think natural phenomena may be legitimately explained: supernatural causation and ascribing purpose to natural phenomena have been dropped in favor of blind, boring, physical causation. Finally, we might speak of the disenchantment of the world in terms of an inward turn, where the experiences of spirits, demons, gods, and moral forces are recast as psychological or even psychopathological conditions.[3] In short, nearly every account of the world's disenchantment construes it as a kind of intellectual pruning or subtraction. Gods are reduced to heavenly bodies mechanically tracing elliptical orbits. Visions of Athena or the archangel Michael are reconceived as hallucinations or tricks of the light.

Weber is making a point about cultural shifts, but individuals can also make the transition from enchantment to disenchantment, as we see in the case of Tara Thornton. Tara's mother, Lettie Mae, has apparently been cured of her alcoholism after receiving an exorcism from the fake witch doctor, Miss Jeanette, who tells Tara that she's possessed by a demon even more powerful and dangerous than her mother's.[4] After some hesitation, Tara pays Miss Jeanette to perform an exorcism on *her*. So far we're squarely in the realm of the enchanted—witch doctors, demons, and soul possession. But shortly after the ceremony Tara discovers that Miss Jeanette is a charlatan who induced visions of a demon by feeding her peyote. Witch doctors and demons are found to be *nothing but* frauds and hallucinations.

Nearly every theorist of modernity, including Weber, cites science as the chief engine of disenchantment: scientific explanations eclipse supernatural and nonnatural modes of explanation. Shamans, demonic possession, astrology, alchemy, divine intervention, and signs—what C. S. Lewis (1898–1963) called "the discarded image"—are replaced with blind, physical causes in coordination with ironclad or probabilistic laws.[5] Science can even tell us how hallucinogenic drugs might lead someone to think she's seeing demons.

Yet before there was science there was philosophy. The Greek philosopher Thales (ca. 624–546 B.C.E.) offered the first rational explanation of how the universe and its many features came to be. While his explanation isn't satisfying—he claims that the Earth and the heavens arose out of *water*—he at least attempted to give an account of how things came into being without invoking the gods, the way the ancient Greek poets Homer and Hesiod did (both of whom may have lived around the eighth century B.C.E.). Science and philosophy share the belief that we can gain knowledge of the world through our own efforts, using reason rather than relying on revelations vouchsafed by some supernatural being.

In fact, many philosophers endorse "Scientific Naturalism," the belief that the universe consists *entirely* of objects that can be adequately described by the natural sciences. Since physics investigates only objective, nonmental, impersonal, mechanistic facts, some philosophers consider everything that can't be described in those terms as, in the words of the philosopher Frank Jackson, "putative" or conjectural.[6] Some of these philosophers believe that the aim of philosophy should be to explain or redescribe the world of our experience in terms derived from the natural sciences. Terms like *ethics*, *consciousness*, *free will*, or *reference* do not belong to the world investigated by natural science, so many Scientific Naturalists would like to redescribe these phenomena in terms that are more amenable to scientific investigation, such as *cause* or *force*.

While many of us aren't ready to embrace every part of Scientific Naturalism's agenda, we do tend to act like scientific naturalists when confronted with claims about certain kinds of phenomena. For example, if a friend tells you she's seen a ghost, you'll probably think she's lying or you'll try to explain away her experience as some sort of neurophysiological or environmental anomaly. In a similar way, Tara discovered that her alleged demon was merely a hallucination.

Perhaps the belief in vampires can be explained away in naturalistic terms. In 1998 Juan Gomez-Alonso published an article in the academic journal *Neurology* arguing that so-called vampires share many properties exhibited by people with rabies.[7] Those who are infected can be violent, suffer insomnia and muscle spasms, and even spit up blood. Their paroxysms can be triggered by strong sensory stimuli, including—you guessed it—exposure to bright lights and the smell of garlic. Gomez-Alonso's research even correlates the historical resurgence of vampire myths with communities experiencing outbreaks of rabies.

Animating the Dead

Gomez-Alonso, a working scientist, is (like most of us) a Scientific Naturalist about vampires: vampires are not real, and if the term *vampire* refers to anything at all, it's probably to those poor folks infected with rabies in the eighteenth century. But Charlaine Harris's fictional world differs from our own: in this world a girl named Sookie lives with her grandmother (at least until her grandmother is murdered) in a small Louisiana town called Bon Temps. And in this fictional world there are not just people with rabies, but actual vampires. While neither Sookie nor vampires exist in our world, the possibility of Sookie, her brother, Jason, her grandmother, and the fictional town of Bon Temps are all compatible with our scientific worldview (ignoring for the moment Sookie's mind-reading abilities and fairy lineage). But the vampires described by Harris don't fit comfortably with our current scientific understanding. Vampires are extremely long-lived (potentially immortal), allergic to sunlight, and dependent on a diet of blood or its less-than-satisfactory synthetic alternative, TrueBlood (TruBlood in the HBO series). Vampire Bill reveals to Sookie that he has no brain waves, no heart beat, no need to breathe, and no electrical impulses in his body—"what animates you no longer animates me."[8]

Sookie seems to accept a version of Scientific Naturalism when early in their relationship she asks Bill,

> Sookie: What does animate you, then? Blood? How do you digest it if nothing works?
>
> Bill: Magic.
>
> Sookie: Come on, Bill. I may look naive, but I'm not.
>
> Bill: You think that it is not magic that keeps you alive? Just because you understand the mechanics of how something works doesn't make it any less of a miracle—which is just another word for magic. We are all kept alive by magic, Sookie. My magic is just a little different from yours, that's all.
>
> Sookie: I think we need to stop seeing each other.[9]

Is Bill's appeal to magic a reasonable response to Sookie's question? Obviously the appeal to magic is laughable to the Scientific Naturalist; that's precisely the sort of talk with which our culture has become gradually disenchanted. For Scientific Naturalists, appeals to "magic" or "miracles" are tantamount to a failure to offer any explanation at all. Yet before we consider the Scientific Naturalist's case, let's attempt to come up with a generous interpretation of Bill's remarks.

Bill might be suggesting that science lacks the resources to explain something like life. In particular, his claim could be that science would fail to explain the phenomenon of life even if it had a full grasp of life's underlying mechanics, so that even a complete scientific understanding of how Sookie's physiology works would still leave some vital remainder unexplained. If so, there would then be a sense in which "magic"—that is, some remainder that eludes scientific explanation—might be said to keep her alive. But what sort of remainder might Bill have in mind? Perhaps something like *consciousness*.

Beginning in the eighteenth century and continuing through the first third of the twentieth century, a debate raged between two opposing views of the phenomenon of life. One camp consisted of the mechanists who, in line with the goals of Scientific Naturalism, attempted to define *life* exclusively in terms of biomechanical organization, the physiological "machinery" of the living being. The vitalists, on the other hand, argued against the reduction of life to its underlying physical mechanisms. They believed that consciousness—or some other magical, holistic, "vital force"—animates otherwise dead matter and distinguishes living things from nonliving things. Bill sounds like he could be a vitalist. If so, his commitment to vitalism might be explained by the fact that he was vampirized in the 1860s, during one of the heydays of this intellectual movement.[10]

Many philosophers have doubted whether science could ever adequately explain conscious experience. Perhaps the most vocal contemporary advocate of the irreducibility of consciousness is the contemporary philosopher John Searle.

Searle grants that the Scientific Naturalist has succeeded in accounting for some phenomena, like heat and color, in terms of underlying, scientifically accessible mechanisms. Heat is nothing but the kinetic energy of molecular movements, and color is nothing but a range on the wavelength spectrum that happens to be accessible to animal light receptors. On the other hand, he argues that no similar redescription of the phenomenon of consciousness is available to the Scientific Naturalist. Searle claims that "a perfect science of the brain would still not lead to an ontological reduction of consciousness in the way that our present science can reduce heat, solidity, color, or sound."[11] In other words, while heat may be nothing more than kinetic energy, consciousness is not the same thing as its underlying neurobiology. Why does Searle think this?

In a paper titled "What Is It Like to Be a Bat?" the philosopher Thomas Nagel argues that science will always fail to explain consciousness.[12] Science explains phenomena by locating them within a causal web, relating them as effects to causes that precede them. Yet any such explanation will miss the essential what-it-feels-like, qualitative, subjective aspect of consciousness. Nagel imagines that one day science might have a perfect grasp of bat neurophysiology or the workings of a bat's brain. Yet even if the brain is the seat of consciousness, a mechanical description of its workings will still miss the subjective experience of what it feels like to be a bat, let's say a *vampire* bat. We can figure out how bat sonar works, but that doesn't tell us what it *feels like* to navigate a forest by means of it. If we can't give an account of consciousness in scientific terms, then perhaps Bill is right to argue that just because "you understand the mechanics of how something works doesn't make it"—in this case, life or consciousness—"any less of a miracle." To the extent that life is bound up with consciousness, it's a miracle because science is unable to explain how it works, how we can *feel* anything at all.

But if Bill is skeptical about reducing consciousness to neurophysiology, his skepticism is far more radical than either Searle's or Nagel's. Searle still thinks that consciousness has a biological basis (no brain, no consciousness) and that it *depends on* the underlying neurophysiology. He would strongly object to Bill's characterization of consciousness as "magical" or "miraculous." In addition, Bill seems to imagine consciousness as borne by some nonphysical life force that *animates* the brain and the body. His description of this life-enabling force recalls the dualism of René Descartes (1596–1650), an early modern philosopher who argued that mind and body were separate, self-sufficient substances. In our disenchanted age, many philosophers, including Searle, have come to regard theories that imply the existence of nonphysical substances as extremely implausible and frankly, to use Sookie's term, "naive."

In any case, it seems that Bill unfairly changes the subject on Sookie. Even if we grant that consciousness is mysterious, Sookie wasn't asking about *that* when she posed the question "What does animate you, then? Blood? How do you digest it if nothing works?" Science's inability to explain consciousness really doesn't have much in common with Bill's inability to explain vampire physiology: digestion isn't as exotic as consciousness. Vampires seem structurally similar to us—they can talk, walk, and have sex. But they do so without electrical neural impulses, blood circulation, or respiration. Shouldn't science be able to explain *that*? Consciousness may be a mystery, maybe for some even a miracle, but the bare facts of metabolism or digestion aren't.

Imagine you go to an auto mechanic and are astonished to discover that he or she doesn't know how an engine works. The mechanic then retorts that you shouldn't be that surprised because, after all, physicists don't really understand how to reconcile all of the fundamental forces within string theory. What an unacceptable response! Bill pulls a similar intellectual bait-and-switch on Sookie. She wants a window into the basics of vampire physiology—after all, the Japanese managed to create synthetic blood, a feat that implies some understanding of such matters—and she gets a lecture on the mind-body problem.

The Heart of the Matter

But what's really at the heart of Sookie's question? Was she really just concerned with reconciling vampire physiology with Scientific Naturalism? Sookie's anatomical worries appear to be stand-ins for a more serious set of moral and existential misgivings. She responds to Bill's appeal to magic by announcing, "I think we need to stop seeing each other." But who breaks up with someone for evading a question about how his body works?

When Bill, understandably upset, presses Sookie to explain why she's ending their relationship, she responds:

> Because you don't breathe. You don't have any electrical whatever-it-is. Your friends would like nothing more than to rip my throat out. . . . Bill, the night before last I had to bury my bloody clothes because I didn't want my grandma to find out I was almost killed. And tonight I was almost killed again. Why on earth *would* I continue seeing you?[13]

Sookie is afraid that she doesn't understand how Bill's heart works. Yet this is not the Scientific Naturalist's point about anatomy. Sookie isn't worried about disentangling the mysterious phenomena of life or vampire digestion. Sookie's concerns about the mechanics of Bill's body flag a whole different set of worries about the kind of *person* he is, about the kinds of activities vampires engage in, and about what these activities reveal about who or what they are. These are existential questions, not scientific ones.

In the aftermath of World War II, the philosopher Jean-Paul Sartre (1905–1980) popularized existentialism with his declarations that "existence precedes essence" and that "man is nothing more than the sum of his actions."[14] What he meant was that there is no given human nature or essence that defines who and what we are. Nor did he believe there was any God to determine that for us. Without a task given to us in advance by a Creator, Sartre believed we are "condemned to be free."[15] The only meaning our lives can have will come through the kind of person we freely choose to be, along with our freely chosen values and obligations. One might choose to be a lover, a firefighter, a hedonist, an artist, a civil rights activist, or any number of other possibilities that in Sartre's terminology would be called our "project." For Sartre your project determines the kind of person you become, the nature that you create for yourself.

Only we ourselves can freely define ourselves by our choices. We are only what we will ourselves to be. We can, however, flee our freedom in a couple of ways. First, we can pretend that we're governed by external constraints, such as some purpose we believe has been assigned to us by our Creator. Second, and more important, even if we deny that we have a God-given essence, we might still see ourselves as governed by a set of internal constraints—desires, passions, or feelings. But Sartre's conception of freedom is radical, for it implies that we're free from both internal and external constraints. "I can neither seek within myself the true condition which will impel me to act," he wrote, "nor apply to a system of ethics for concepts which will permit me to act."[16] Passions, desires, and feelings have no power to move us without our consent and so can never be offered as an excuse, according to Sartre. "The existentialist does not believe in the power of passion."[17]

Those who pretend they're not really free are acting in "bad faith." Tara exhibits bad faith when she prefers to believe that magic cured her anger issues and gets enraged when she discovers that she was tricked. But it was her choice to believe the scam. More important, whether she chooses to acknowledge it or not, she actually changed her attitude on her own. She should now accept full responsibility for her current choice to return to her old ways. She alone is ultimately responsible for her behavior and feelings. In Sartre's language, she's still condemned to be free.

So why does Sookie threaten to leave Bill? Vampires superficially resemble human beings, but they work differently. They don't breathe: it is not oxygen that sustains them, but human blood. And the need to drink human blood equips them with fangs, capable of piercing and subduing human flesh. But the vampires of Harris's world work differently in another sense. Before meeting Sookie, Bill seemed to spend most of his time playing the Nintendo Wii. Other vampires are depicted spending an inordinate amount of time playing Yahtzee. Yet these leisurely activities are not rich enough to define a life or make it meaningful. Some vampires, including Bill's friends, live for the momentary satisfaction that comes from feeding. But a meaningful life can't be built out of merely haphazard accretions of pleasure.

As the series unfolds, however, we discover more substantial vampire activities: the vampires have a complex hierarchy of sheriffs and their underlings, magistrates, public relations managers, queens, kings, and council members. Yet it is not clear that these roles are *freely* entered into. The vampires appear to act not so much out of obligations they freely embrace, but because they are compelled to act—perhaps out of fear or the inescapable demands of loyalty to their makers. If Sartre is correct, human beings are different. Even if we act out of desire and feeling, we could have freely chosen not to do so.

When Sookie wonders whether Bill works like she does, she's probably not really worried about the details of vampire digestion. More likely, she's fretting about the kinds of motivations from which vampire Bill is capable of acting and what that says about him as a person. Had she read her Sartre, she might have asked: Can he act from obligations freely chosen? Is he condemned to be free like me?

After discovering in *Definitely Dead*, the sixth book of the Southern Vampire Mysteries, that Bill seduced her on orders from the queen of Louisiana, Sookie forever after distrusts his proclamations of true love. She suspects that the seemingly limited range of vampire motivations renders Bill incapable of loving as humans do. If passions and feelings drive vampires without their choosing to embrace those passions as a part of a project, they're not existentially free in the way that human beings are, notwithstanding their mysterious physiology. More urgently, this implies that Bill is not free to choose Sookie.

Blood Ties and Freedom

If these are Sookie's concerns, they appear to be unfounded. Let's look at three illustrations. First, vampires are conscious and thus, according to Sartre's view, condemned to be free just like human beings. That some vampires freely choose projects that Sookie abhors does not diminish their freedom or their responsibility for creating their own essence. When Bill explains how his vampire friend Malcolm can easily torture and dispatch his former human lover, Jerry, he presupposes that Malcolm could have done otherwise and thus has Sartrean freedom:

> Sookie: They are all so mean, so . . .
>
> Bill: Evil. Yes, they are. They share a nest. And when vampires share a nest, they become more cruel, more vicious. They become laws unto themselves. Whereas vampires such as I, when we live alone, we are much more likely to hold on to some semblance of our former humanity.[18]

Not only can vampires decide to live alone, but they can also choose whether to engage in vicious projects like torture, bloodletting, or violent sex. After all, labels like "evil" and "cruel" are not appropriately applied to unfree beings: moral condemnation implies that the wrongdoer could have done otherwise.

Second, in *From Dead to Worse*, the eighth book of the Southern Vampire Mysteries, Sookie herself attempts to deny her freedom by pretending that she has acted under compulsion. Sookie and Eric Northman have established a blood tie, causing her to second-guess her reasons for wanting to help him. She responds to his gratitude for saving his life during the explosion at the vampire summit by trying to evade responsibility for her own choices.

> [Sookie:] "We do have the blood tie thing going."
>
> [Eric:] "That's not why you came to wake me, first of all, the day the hotel blew up."[19]

Eric implicitly suggests that in denying her freedom Sookie is acting in bad faith, lying both to herself and to him. Yet that shows that vampires *themselves* distinguish between acts made under a compulsion and those made by free choice, in which case freedom must be a genuine possibility for vampires as well.

Sometimes characters really do appear to have fallen under a spell that deprives them of freedom and agency: vampires can glamour most human beings, and Maryann the maenad can bring human beings under her control. But a blood tie between a vampire and a human being seems different, more like a desire that can be resisted. Indeed, both Bill and Eric become fascinated with Sookie in part because of her unique ability to resist the powers of vampire compulsion. They are attracted to her freedom.

Finally, even the hierarchy of vampiric occupations appears open to choice. When in *Dead as a Doornail*, the fifth book of the Southern Vampire Mysteries, Eric initially regains his memories of his tender courtship of Sookie, he struggles to reconcile his past deeds with his current project of being a ruthless independent sheriff. In *Dead and Gone*, the ninth book of the Southern Vampire Mysteries, his initial shock that he offered to give up all his power as sheriff to make a life with her disappears when he remembers how happy they had been together. Sookie frets that she can't trust her feelings because—again—she doesn't understand the possible sway of their blood tie on her emotions. In contrast, Eric's actions to shore up his power base and to woo her reveal his new project of bringing together Eric the lover and Eric the mighty. He refuses to be limited by his past, and he projects himself toward a new future with Sookie. Eric's literal pulse may be silent, but his freely chosen actions are the measure and expression of his heart.

Ultimately, Sookie discovers that vampires are free and responsible just like human beings. What will re-enchant her universe and allow her to find the sublime in the ordinary is the magic of meeting a heart like her own, whether that heart beats or not. In the end, it's the ordinary moments of courtship that re-enchant Sookie's world, as she comments to herself after reuniting with Eric, "This was the real treat, or at least one of the real treats—having someone with whom to share the day's events. Eric was a good listener, at least in his postcoital relaxed state."[20] The real flaw in Sookie's relationship with Bill wasn't his different physiology, or the fact that he was unfree. Rather, his freely chosen secretiveness and ulterior motivations doomed their relationship. He wasn't the *kind of person* with whom she could re-enchant the universe, the kind of person moved by reasons that escape scientific explanation—those of the heart.[21]

NOTES

1. Max Weber, "Science as a Vocation," *Daedalus* 87 (1958): 133.

2. Wilfrid Sellars, "Philosophy and the Scientific Image of Man," in *Frontiers of Science and Philosophy*, ed. Robert Garland Colodny (Pittsburgh: Univ. of Pittsburgh Press, 1962), pp. 35–78, www.ditext.com/sellars/psim.html.

3. Charles Taylor, "Buffered and Porous Selves," *Immanent Frame*, September 2, 2008, blogs.ssrc.org/tif/2008/09/02/buffered-and-porous-selves/.

4. Episode 110, "I Don't Wanna Know."

5. C. S. Lewis, *The Discarded Image: An Introduction to Medieval and Renaissance Literature* (Cambridge, UK: Cambridge Univ. Press, 1994).

6. Frank Jackson, *From Metaphysics to Ethics: A Defence of Conceptual Analysis* (Oxford: Oxford Univ. Press, 1998), p. 5.

7. Juan Gomez-Alonso, "Rabies—A Possible Explanation for the Vampire Legend," *Neurology* 51 (1998): 856–859.

8. Episode 103, "Mine."

9. Ibid.

10. For example, in 1858 Rudolph Virchow championed what he called "Modern Vitalism."

11. John R. Searle, *The Rediscovery of the Mind* (Cambridge, MA: MIT Press, 1992), p. 116.

12. Thomas Nagel, "What Is It Like to Be a Bat?" *Philosophical Review* 83 (1974): 435. For more on Nagel and his relevance to *True Blood* and the Southern Vampire Mysteries, see William M. Curtis's chapter in this volume, "'Honey, If We Can't Kill People, What's the Point of Being a Vampire?': Can Vampires Be Good Citizens?"

13. Episode 103, "Mine."

14. Jean-Paul Sartre, *Existentialism and Human Emotions* (New York: Citadel, 2000), pp. 13, 37, 46.

15. Ibid., pp. 23, 52.

16. Ibid., p. 27.

17. Ibid., p. 23.

18. Episode 103, "Mine."

19. Charlaine Harris, *From Dead to Worse* (New York: Ace Books, 2008), p. 56.

20. Charlaine Harris, *Dead and Gone* (New York: Ace Trade, 2009), p. 173.

21. The authors would like to thank Ronald Hall for discussions that greatly influenced the overall shape of this chapter. They would also like to thank the editors for their helpful comments. And last but not least, Susan and Josh wish to thank their respective spouses for their patience during the duration of this project.

KEEPING SECRETS
FROM SOOKIE

Fred Curry

Sookie Stackhouse can't snap trees in two as though they were toothpicks, nor can she tip over trailers. She can't shrug off massive bodily damage, transform into a bird, glamour a person into doing her bidding, or make the people of a small town give in to bestial urges. Nevertheless, in many ways, Sookie is the most powerful character in the *True Blood* series. Her powers are not flashy. In fact, nobody even knows when she is using them, which makes her abilities all the more useful.

Sookie actually has two powers that seem to be related. She is immune to particular supernatural influences, such as glamouring, and, more important, she is an exceedingly strong telepath. Her telepathic senses are so acute that she has more difficulty *blocking out* the thoughts of others than she does "reading" them. Sookie is the knower of secrets. She can know what any human being in her presence is thinking at any time; this ability has saved her life and those of her friends several times over.

The usefulness of Sookie's powers is fairly obvious upon reflection. What might not be so obvious are any possible limitations to her telepathic ability. Can she really take any knowledge she wants from anybody within range? Suppose, for example, that Sookie wanted to know everything that Lafayette Reynolds knows—could she achieve that? Jumping to conclusions here would be a mistake. Sookie can clearly gain particular types of information from Lafayette, such as what he had for breakfast that morning or what he's intending to do later that night, but does her access to that kind of information show that *nothing* in Lafayette's consciousness can be hidden from Sookie? Our question isn't how powerful a telepath Sookie is but whether Lafayette—or anyone else for that matter—could possess any kind of knowledge that even the most powerful telepath couldn't learn using her powers. In other words, could there be anything genuinely private about the contents of our minds if there were real telepaths like Sookie able to break through any human psychological defense? Could there be built-in limitations to telepathy that arise due to the very nature of our minds?

Before we can make progress on this question, we'll need to take a short detour from our main line of investigation and get introduced to a couple of important philosophical ideas. But as Gran Stackhouse might say, "This won't take two shakes of a lamb's tail."

What's It Like to Hear a Dog-Whistle?

Let's put Sookie out of our minds for a moment and focus our attention instead on Sam Merlotte. Let's assume that there's a full moon in the sky and that Sam is unable to restrain himself from shapeshifting into his preferred form, a collie, and going out to explore the woods. Let's also suppose that somebody in the distance blows a dog-whistle. Dog-whistles sound at a pitch that humans can't hear, but Sam can hear it with no difficulty when he's in his dog form. Let's explore all of the facets of this event.

Much of what's going on involves physical objects that interact in ways that could in theory be described by anybody with the right scientific background. Such a description can be given from a "third-person" perspective, meaning a descriptive point of view not specific to any particular person. From this perspective we could describe a causal chain of physical events that lead ultimately to Sam's hearing the sound—the blowing of the whistle, the vibration it causes in the air, the waves formed by this vibration, the contact of these waves with Sam's eardrums, the firing of nerve cells in response to this contact, and as a result the firing of neurons in Sam's brain. With enough information we could give an extremely detailed account that notes the motion of every atom in the causal chain that extends from the blowing of the whistle and the firing of neurons in Sam's brain. Or we could just say something as simple as "Somebody blew a whistle, and Sam heard it."

But can even the most detailed description of this chain of causes tell us everything about the event? No, because what this account is unable to capture is the quality of Sam's subjective *conscious experience* when hearing the dog-whistle, that is, *what it's like to hear a dog-whistle*.[1] We still would not know what it's really like for Sam to hear the dog-whistle; we wouldn't know the quality of his experience. Sam possesses a type of information unavailable to everyone else who may witness this event, even if they make precise measurements of all of its objective elements, such as the air particles set in motion when the whistle is blown. Sam knows something that no human being can—*what a dog-whistle sounds like to a dog*. Such qualitative conscious experiences are known by philosophers as *qualia*.[2] Qualia is a plural term. When we speak of a single qualitative conscious experience, we use the term *quale*.

Even though physical descriptions don't *seem* to entail qualia, that doesn't make it self-evidently true that qualia must be nonphysical. There are indeed many philosophers who think that qualia must be something nonphysical. But other philosophers believe that qualia *are* physical; it's just that they are inaccessible to minds other than the one experiencing them. Some of these philosophers even think that once we fully understand the workings of the brain, an objective description of a brain state would entail a description of the person's subjective experiences. If they're right, then Sookie's telepathy wouldn't provide her with any information about the content of other minds that nontelepaths couldn't theoretically learn through scientific measurements of brain activity. (Of course, we might have to wait a while for technology to become sufficiently sophisticated.) But let's proceed on the assumption that Sookie does have access to information about other minds in a way that other human beings don't. Would there be any built-in limitations to her powers?

Hunting the Elusive Quale

Qualia *seem* to represent a special kind of knowledge that's directly accessible only to one person, namely the person to whose mind they belong, the person immediately conscious of them. But maybe it's not yet clear why—at least in a world without telepathy—we think of qualia as private, in our minds but inaccessible to others. Considering our reasons for regarding qualia as private should help to sharpen our understanding of these elusive entities.

Suppose Sam wanted to describe what hearing the dog-whistle was like to the waitress Arlene Fowler. What could he tell her? He could describe the physical events in the way we did earlier, from the blowing of the whistle to the motion of the atoms, but we already know that an objective third-person description can't convey what it's *like* to hear the dog-whistle. Maybe he could say something like "It's kind of painful, a higher pitch than the high frequency whine that you sometimes hear when the television or another piece of electronics is malfunctioning." He might even come up with a more clever use of similes or turns of phrase to explain his experience to her. But all Arlene knows at this point is what the experience she would label as "pain" is like to her, not the experience of pain that is peculiar to experiencing the sound of a dog-whistle. And although she knows that some sounds are "higher" than others, the only pitches she can ever really *know* are those that she has experienced herself.

It might be tempting to think that the only reason Arlene could not know what it's like to hear the dog-whistle is that she is unable to hear the same frequencies that Sam can when he is in dog form. But this would be a mistake. Qualitative experiences are necessarily incommunicable. You can never know exactly what my subjective experience of eating chocolate ice cream is like, for example, even if you've eaten plenty of chocolate ice cream yourself. To help make this barrier in communication clearer, let's look at a variation of an argument first advanced by the philosopher John Locke (1632–1704), the inverted spectrum argument.[3]

First, imagine yourself looking at something green, and then fix firmly in your mind what the quale of that experience is like. Next, imagine that Jason Stackhouse experiences the color green in exactly the same way you do. In other words, *what it is like* for you to see green is exactly what it is like for Jason to see green. Now imagine yourself seeing something red, and again fix in your mind what that experience is like. Finally, imagine that the quale you have when seeing the color *red* is exactly what Tara Thornton experiences when she sees something *green*. Tara and Jason therefore experience the color green differently, but as we'll see, they have no way of expressing this difference to each other.

Suppose that Jason and Tara are talking to each other during the Christmas season one year. Jason points at a storefront window and says, "Look at that artificial Christmas tree! It's as green as Astroturf. Maybe Sookie will forgive me for insulting Bill if I get it for her." Tara responds by saying, "Sookie doesn't want some fake-ass tree no matter how green it is, and you're crazy if you think you can just buy her forgiveness."

Now notice that while both Jason and Tara use the same color word ("green") to describe the tree, they experience the color of the tree in different ways. Jason experiences the tree's color in exactly the same way you do, but Tara experiences it the same way you would if it were what you call "red." Although they have no difficulty talking to each other about the tree and making themselves understood, they're experiencing completely different qualia. It follows that each knows something about the tree that the other can't know, namely, how it appears from his or her subjective point of view.

Communicating the difference in their experiences isn't just difficult—it's impossible. Both Jason and Tara learned the word *green* by observing the behavior of others. Perhaps Jason's mother pointed to the grass and said "green," and then to leaves and said "green," and then to Astroturf, and so on until Jason came to associate the word *green* with the quale or experience of color that all of those objects produce in him. He learned other words in much the same way. The same is true for Tara.

Consequently, Tara and Jason would completely agree about which objects should be called green, although their qualia differ and neither has any access to the other's conscious experience. They each know how the word *green* is used, what types of items are described as green, and what it is like to experience green for themselves. But they have no way of knowing whether their own experiences are at all like the experiences of anybody else viewing the same objects. This is not simply a quirk of language. Everything Jason and Tara know about green things comes from observing the behavior of others and their own conscious experiences, which now appear to be entirely private.

Our own conscious experience seems to consist of what we know most directly and surely, but at the same time this experience is impossible for others to verify and for us to communicate to them. So, in terms of at least one type of knowledge, our direct firsthand experience of our minds' own qualia, philosophers often argue that our minds are completely isolated from one another. This isolation is called *privacy of mind*.

But of course, the philosophers who have argued for privacy of mind in the past were never confronted with a telepath like Sookie. We might agree that for beings such as ourselves, the qualia of others are forever hidden, but is such knowledge hidden from Sookie as well? Or are there truly no secrets from Sookie?

A Slow Day at Merlotte's

Since it will again be useful to have a concrete example, let's suppose that Sookie is waiting tables at Merlotte's during a slow lunch shift. She's serving coffee to Maxine Fortenberry, her only customer at the moment. Maxine's reading a tabloid article, the title of which shouts out in large boldfaced letters: "Get Rich with Your Own Personal Astrological Stock Adviser!"

The article claims that growing numbers of people are achieving financial independence through stock market investments suggested by their personal astrologers. Best of all, these astrologers charge only ten percent of what you gain. Their work is guaranteed, since if you don't earn money, they don't get paid. Maxine is reading intently.

Sookie, even without the benefit of her telepathic powers, knows that Maxine is a fervent believer in astrology and can see that she's wholly engrossed in the article. But even in a world full of vampires, shapeshifters, werewolves, maenads, and fairies, Sookie still retains enough skepticism to recognize that astrology is nonsense. As she mentally fires off a crack about fools and their money, she suddenly wonders what it would be *like* to believe in astrology. It just seems like such nonsense to her! What could stars, so many light-years away that they might not even exist anymore, possibly have to do with the

Dow Jones industrial average? What would it really feel like to believe that kind of stuff? Curious, she dives into Maxine's mind. What would Sookie experience? What would she learn as a result?

For the purposes of our discussion we need consider only two possibilities: First, while reading Maxine's mind, Sookie could become so caught up in her thoughts that she herself becomes a believer in astrology. Alternatively, she could retain her skepticism during the time she's reading Maxine's mind. Given the setup, it must be one or the other. Sookie either retains her doubt or she does not. Since there are only two possibilities, let's examine both of them in turn.

Let's first suppose that while in Maxine's mind Sookie's consciousness is so altered that she's totally convinced by the article. That, of course, is what would have to happen in order for Sookie to have the same qualitative experience as Maxine. It turns out that Maxine is not only reading but also thinking about hiring an astrologer as a stock adviser, recalling a childhood memory about how impressed she was by an astrological reading at the circus, feeling greedy and excited at the prospect of all of that money she's going to make, and so on. Let's suppose that as long as Sookie applies her telepathic powers to Maxine's mind, all of these conscious experiences are not only Maxine's but Sookie's as well. For the time being, Sookie's qualia are identical to Maxine's.

But there seems to be a problem. Sookie can know what it is like to have someone else's conscious experience only if it is Sookie herself who's doing the knowing. But while looking into Maxine's mind, Sookie seems to have lost herself, since her own subjective consciousness is no longer hers but just a copy of Maxine's. Before she began to read Maxine's mind, Sookie had memories, values, and beliefs that were completely different from her gullible tabloid-reading customer. Sookie *doesn't* believe in astrology. She *wouldn't* feel excitement at the prospect of getting rich by hiring an astrologer. That just isn't who Sookie is—and, therefore, whatever is "sharing" Maxine's consciousness is in a very real sense not Sookie Stackhouse during that time. It's really just a duplication of Maxine's consciousness, indistinguishable from the original. So if our first possibility is true and Sookie's experiences become the same as Maxine's for as long as she's reading her, then Sookie loses her own character while inside Maxine's mind. But then *Sookie* herself is actually never aware of Maxine's experiences at all. It is no longer Sookie who is experiencing what it's like to be Maxine—it's a consciousness with a psychological character entirely different from Sookie's.

Perhaps somebody would object that although Sookie would lose herself *during* the telepathic experience, she could remember the experience after she exits Maxine's mind and in this way know what it is like to believe in astrology. But that only pushes the problem one step backward. Sookie's memories are subject to the same dilemma that her telepathic experience was subject to in the first place. Either Sookie's own psychology and personality are swept aside when she remembers her telepathic experience inside Maxine's mind, or they're retained. If her experiences are just like Maxine's, then Sookie's own psychology disappears and the problem pops back up again as quickly as a vampire accidentally staked with Formica. If not, then the situation amounts to accepting the second possibility, which we'll now consider.

The second possibility is that when Sookie enters Maxine's mind she doesn't lose herself but retains her own psychological characteristics, including her skepticism about astrology. But this possibility has its own problems. Imagine that Sookie's psychology remains intact during her journey into the mind of Maxine. That would mean that during her telepathic excursion, her own consciousness is active and in some way *combined* with Maxine's. The result is that Sookie doesn't know what it is like to be *Maxine* while believing in astrology. After all, Maxine isn't experiencing a *mixed* consciousness at all. She isn't even aware of Sookie's telepathic intrusion. While Sookie experiences whatever it's like to disbelieve in astrology while peering into a mind that has unshakable faith that astrology is true, Maxine experiences only her unshakable faith.

The upshot is that if Sookie's conscious states are different from Maxine's, then she doesn't *really* know what it is like to be Maxine. On the other hand, if her conscious experiences *are* the same as Maxine's, then those experiences aren't really being known by *Sookie*, since the Sookie we know has for all intents and purposes left the building, along with all of the memories and psychological characteristics that define her as a distinct individual.

The Final Nail in the Coffin

In the event that this argument seems like some sort of logical glamouring, consider yourself. We can even find it impossible to access the qualia of *our own* experiences as our psychologies change. Try to remember something that you enjoy now but had to acquire a taste for. For my part, I'll remember what it's like to drink coffee. Perhaps that example will work for you as well.[4]

When I think of how I experienced coffee recently, my mouth waters a bit and I wish that it wasn't too late in the evening to go and pour myself a cup. But I also remember that I didn't always like the taste of coffee. In fact, I can remember that when I was a child, my father gave in to my pleadings for a taste, and I regretted it immediately. Repulsed by the taste, I thought that my parents must be crazy for ordering the stuff every time we went out to eat. But while my memory of this event seems to be intact and I can remember that I didn't like the taste of coffee when I was a child, I cannot recall the qualia of tasting coffee and *not* enjoying the taste.[5]

This isn't surprising. After all, I now *like* the flavor of coffee. Nevertheless, when I was a child, just thinking about the taste of coffee would make me shiver with disgust. Now

I crave what once disgusted me. Clearly my qualitative conscious experience of the same event, drinking coffee, is now very different from how I experienced it as a child, although the rest of the memory seems to have remained intact. One likely reason may be that we interpret sensations (including our remembered sensations) through the complex maze of our own unique psychologies, which are shaped by different past experiences. My psychology has changed since I was a child and now interacts with coffee stimulus in a way that I find pleasurable. Twenty-five years ago this wasn't the case. Yet, if access to the qualia of *my own* past can change so drastically during what is hopefully still the first half of my life that I cannot access them, how could someone hope to access the qualia of a completely different individual?

So if you ever find yourself in Bon Temps talking to a fetching blond waitress with an unusual name, rest assured that even if the inclination to read your mind should overtake her, there are some things about you she can never know. Most important, she'll never know what it's like to experience things as you.

NOTES

1. This line, which provides the title of this section, is a deliberate homage to Thomas Nagel's famous philosophical article, "What Is It Like to Be a Bat?" *Philosophical Review* 83 (1974): 435–450. For more on Nagel and his relevance to *True Blood*, see Susan Peppers-Bates and Joshua Rust's chapter in this volume, "A Vampire's Heart Has Its Reasons That Scientific Naturalism Can't Understand," and William M. Curtis's chapter, "'Honey, If We Can't Kill People, What's the Point of Being a Vampire?': Can Vampires Be Good Citizens?"

2. The modern use of this word was first introduced by the great pragmatic philosopher C. I. Lewis. See his *Mind and the World Order: Outline of a Theory of Knowledge* (New York: Scribner's Sons, 1929).

3. John Locke, *Essay Concerning Human Understanding* (Boston: Adamant Media Corporation, 2001), p. 435.

4. It turns out that while I originally thought the coffee example was my own, the famous philosopher of mind Daniel C. Dennett used the example of coffee with the idea of changing tastes in his paper "Quining Qualia," in *Mind and Cognition: A Reader*, ed. by William G. Lycan (Oxford: Basil Blackwell, 1999), pp. 519–547. I am making a slightly different point here. Dennett argues that in such a case it could be that either the quale

of the coffee has changed or the standards of taste for that person have changed (or both). The qualia I am referring to, however, relate to the entire conscious experience, which includes both the tasting of the coffee and either liking it or not liking it. Since I am referring to the entire qualitative experience of what it is to taste coffee as a person with particular tastes, a change from disliking coffee to liking coffee (since these are themselves experiences) indicates a qualitative change in the experience as a whole.

5. Or think of a vampire like Bill Compton, who perhaps can no longer enjoy his favorite foods from 150 years ago because since then not only his psychology but also his physiology has undergone a dramatic change as a result of becoming a vampire. He might also not be able to recall the qualia of liking crawfish or sweet-potato pie or whatever food may have been popular in Bon Temps back in antebellum days, while nonetheless remembering *that* he did like them.

VAMPIRES, WEREWOLVES, AND SHAPESHIFTERS

The More They Change, the More They Stay the Same

Sarah Grubb

The way vampires are treated in the Sookie–verse has a lot to do with what others consider them to be. In *Dead until Dark*, the first book of the Southern Vampire Mysteries by Charlaine Harris, Sookie reports, "The politically correct theory, the one the vamps themselves publicly backed, had it that [vampires were the] victim of a virus that left [them] apparently dead for a couple of days and thereafter allergic to sunlight, silver, and garlic."[1] Some characters, like Sookie, consider these new creatures to be *people* at their core, deserving of consideration and respect. Many others in Bon Temps simply consider them to be monsters with pointy fangs, no longer having any semblance of humanity within them. To get a better grip on what's at stake, let's see what some philosophical theories about the nature of personal identity might have to say about these supernatural creatures.

Becoming a Vamp: "Vampires Are Not Supposed to Say 'Uh-Oh.'"

We first meet Bill Compton as he takes a seat at Merlotte's Bar and Grill to order a bottle of TruBlood (called TrueBlood in the Southern Vampire Mysteries). His presence is noticed as soon as he enters the establishment, as he is the first vampire the town has ever seen. Indeed, Sookie remarks to Bill, "You're our first."[2] As Sookie describes his appearance in *Dead until Dark,* "He was a little under six feet, I estimated. He had thick brown hair, combed straight back and brushing his collar, and his long sideburns seemed curiously old-fashioned. He was pale, of course; hey, he was dead, if you believed the old tales."[3] We learn that Bill had been a husband and father in the town of Bon Temps before he was called away to fight in the Civil War. Sometime after the war Bill was transformed into a vampire by Lorena, at whose hands he died and was restored to "life" as a vampire.

Another vampire whose transformation we witness on *True Blood* is Jessica Hamby. After killing Longshadow in order to save Sookie's life, Bill was ordered to atone for his deed by creating a new vampire from a human being—something he'd never done before. His unlucky victim was seventeen-year-old Jessica. Our early impression of Jessica is that she's a modest, proper southern girl. Although roughed up from her kidnapping, she was dressed neatly and prayed earnestly as she faced death. But after becoming a vampire, she experiences some significant changes. No longer a demure and outwardly pious teenage girl, Jessica becomes rebellious, exhibiting what she calls "vampire impulse control issues."[4]

Bill and Jessica undergo significant changes during the course of their existence. How do these two characters retain a sense of self? Are Bill and Jessica the same individuals now as they were before they became vampires? For some religiously inclined people, the answer might depend on whether Bill and Jessica as vampires still possess the same *souls* they had when they were human beings.[5] We know that at least one religious group, the Fellowship of the Sun, emphatically denies that vampires have souls, but it's not at all clear how they think they can know this alleged fact. And, of course, many people, including many philosophers, are skeptical about the very existence of souls, given the absence of any scientific evidence for these elusive and intangible entities. Philosophical theories have tended to look elsewhere for an explanation of how we can still be the same individuals despite all of the physical and psychological changes we undergo throughout our lives. If we do retain our personal identities over time, what is it about us that stays the same through all of these changes? More particularly, what, if anything, connects the human and vampire "lives" of Bill and Jessica so that despite everything they've become they're still the same individuals?

The Bodily Theory: "You're Alive!" . . . "Well, Technically, No"

The bodily theory of personal identity offers one possible answer. It says that we retain our identities across time despite all of the changes that we undergo, as long as we keep the same body for the whole time. As we grow up, our body changes; it grows taller and wider, and sometimes it even gets broken in places. But despite all of these changes, it's still the same body that we started out with, just reshaped a bit. It's the essential element that remains despite all of the other changes we undergo. Our personal identity is equivalent to our body.

It seems like our bodies are one of the few things that stay with us throughout our entire lives, so the bodily theory might initially seem compelling. But it runs up against some problems. Do our bodies actually remain the same? Not really. And it's not only the shape of our bodies that changes over time; the very atoms and molecules out of which they're made also change. Our bodies shed cells constantly and ingest new material in the form of nutrients with every meal that we consume. If our human bodies don't really remain the same throughout our lives, how can the bodily theory account for our personal identity? And if the bodily theory can't account for the personal identity of human beings, how can it account for Bill and Jessica?

Bill began as a human being, with a body that experienced normal growth until his transformation into a vampire. The same is true for Jessica. When they became vampires, their bodies ceased to be alive. Their organs shut down, their cells died, and eventually all of their bodily systems ceased to function. If the bodies of regular human beings undergo too much change over time to satisfy the bodily theory, what are we to say about Bill and Jessica after the even more extreme changes in composition their bodies underwent when they transformed into vampires? If the bodily theory can't account for human personal identity, then it seems even less promising as an explanation of how Bill and Jessica retain their identities after becoming vampires. Although their vampire bodies may look the same as their human bodies, they're no longer the same. Lacking a pulse and brainwaves, they're technically no longer even alive. Describing the process of making a vampire to Sookie, Bill explains, "I would have to drain you, at one sitting or over two or three days, to the point of your death, then give you my blood. You would lie like a corpse for about forty-eight hours, sometimes as long as three days, then rise and walk at night."[6] After their transformation, vampires have bodies that operate differently from any human body. Instead of eating food, they consume human blood (either real or synthetic). Instead of crying tears, they cry blood. What are we to say of their identities? The drastic changes in Bill and Jessica's bodily composition and function leaves the bodily theory unable to account for how they retain the same personal identities they had before becoming vampires. But it seems as though they are still the same individuals nonetheless. They retain memories of their human lives and still have many aspects of their human personalities. Bill remembers his family and life as a human being and not just as though he were observing *another* person's life. Same for Jessica. So it looks like we need to abandon the bodily theory. Are there any better theories of personal identity?

Memory: "What Animates You No Longer Animates Me"

The memory theory is an account of personal identity proposed by the philosopher John Locke (1632–1704). Locke argued that we retain our identities despite changes over time as long as we retain the memories that connect us to past episodes in our lives. In *An Essay Concerning Human Understanding*, Locke wrote that if one atom of an ordinary object "be taken away, or one new one added, it is no longer the same Mass, or the same Body." But what's true of ordinary objects doesn't hold for living beings—or even, it seems reasonable to assume, for undead creatures like Bill and Jessica. "In the state of living Creatures," Locke argued, "their Identity depends not on a Mass of the same Particles, but on something else."[7] He explains what that something else would be for the category of living creatures he calls persons:

> [T]o find wherein *personal Identity* consists, we must consider what *Person* stands for; which, I think, is a thinking intelligent Being, that has reason and reflection, and can consider it self as it self, the same thinking thing in different times and places. . . . [I]n this alone consists *personal Identity*, i.e., the sameness of a rational Being: And as far as this consciousness can be extended backwards to any past Action or Thought, so far reaches the Identity of that *Person*.[8]

Locke argues that we retain our personal identities despite all of the changes we undergo as long as we carry memories from our past and continue to recognize ourselves in our past actions and experiences. We know that Bill is able to remember his life as a human being. Since Bill can still reflect on that former life and recognize the actions of the human Bill Compton as his own, Locke's memory theory allows us to say that Bill is the same person now, as a vampire, that he was then, as a human. Since Jessica can also remember her life as a human being and even carries grudges against her father for the way he mistreated her human self, she also satisfies Locke's criterion for being the same person she was prior to her transformation.

But there are problems with the memory theory of identity. One difficulty concerns the issue of memory loss. Bill and Jessica haven't experienced memory loss, but another vampire in the Southern Vampire Mysteries has. Bill's sheriff, Eric Northman, suffers memory loss in *Dead to the World*, the fourth book of the Southern Vampire Mysteries. On the way home from a New Year's Eve party at Merlotte's Bar and Grill, Sookie finds Eric running down a road, apparently being chased. She soon discovers that Eric doesn't recognize her and doesn't even remember who he is, although he knows he is a vampire. Despite this development, Sookie and others still regard Eric as the same person that he was before his memory loss. For instance, speaking with Eric while he's in his amnesiac state, Sookie remarks, "I have a brother. I can't remember if you've ever met Jason."[9] Notice that she doesn't say, "You haven't met him," but that's just what she would have said if she thought of this amnesiac person as someone different from the Eric she knew. Eric's memory loss, brought on by a witch's curse, is only temporary. But despite these changes in memory, we still consider Eric to have been Eric all along, just temporarily unable to *remember* who he is. We don't say, "Eric ceased to exist, but then came back into being once his memories returned." But if we think someone can retain his or her identity over time despite memory loss, it follows that identity depends on something *other* than memory and that no one—neither vampire nor human—can retain identity solely as a result of retaining their memories.

Perhaps it isn't memory but psychological continuity, more broadly speaking, that allows us to remain the same person over time.

Psychological Continuity: "I Hate Using the Number Keys to Type"

If we apply the criterion of psychological continuity, our personal identities endure over time by maintaining the same psychological makeup, or at least one that's causally related to our past psychological conditions. According to this view, Bill's present self is the same as his past self just as long as his present psychological state can be explained, at least in large part, as the outcome of an uninterrupted succession of past psychological states.

We might be tempted to think that this is the solution to the problem of explaining how Bill can be the same person despite his transformation into a vampire. After all, what makes Bill unlike many other vampires is that he seems to retain more psychological continuity with his former human self. Delving further, however, we find that this explanation has problems as well. Bill may be *more* psychologically similar to his human self than most vampires, but we see him give in to his darker vampire nature at times. Flashbacks in the second season of *True Blood* show Bill and his maker, Lorena, hunting and feeding on human beings for sport. It doesn't seem that Bill's psychological states as a fledgling vampire resulted from his previous psychological states as a human being, but instead had more to do with the new dark force that lurked inside him. Arguably, Bill already had some aggressive human tendencies within him, but even so, the degree of aggression that vampire Bill displays is way out of proportion to anything he likely exhibited as a human being. Whatever latent human aggression may have surfaced appears to have been greatly intensified by his vampire nature. Even now that Bill is mainstreaming, we see his vampire nature emerge on occasion. In *Dead until Dark*, Bill remarks to Sookie that vampires lack "human values." He explains, "There is something in me that isn't cruel, not murderous, even after all these years. Though I can be both."[10] This is not to deny the many similarities between vampire Bill and his former human self. But his previous psychological state as a human being doesn't seem to be responsible for the homicidal tendencies he acquired when he became a vampire, as the criterion of psychological continuity requires if he's to be regarded as the same person.

Psychological continuity doesn't seem to be a sufficient explanation for how Jessica has retained her personal identity either. The differences in psychological states between Jessica's human and vampire selves are striking. Before Jessica's transformation, she seems to have been a calm, gentle, complacent, and traditional girl. But her newfound vampirism and freedom from the influence of her parents cause her to exhibit a much more rebellious nature. By the end of season 2, she's no longer just feeling violent impulses, but committing actual acts of aggression toward human beings—first Hoyt Fortenberry's mother and then some hapless, horny truck driver. We'll see what happens to Jessica in season 3 of *True Blood*, given the drastic changes she has undergone, but this much is certain: if she's the same person now that she was as a human being, it's not because she satisfies the psychological continuity criterion of identity.

Werewolves and Shapeshifters: "Life Is Just Getting Too Weird Too Fast"

The criterion of psychological continuity isn't helpful when dealing with the personal identity of shapeshifters and werewolves either. Consider Sam Merlotte. Sam has a secret—he's a shapeshifter, a supernatural creature able to transform himself into an animal. Explaining how this transformation occurs, Sam tells Sookie, "I turn into whatever animal I saw before I changed. So I keep a dog book open to a picture of a collie on my coffee table."[11] Shapeshifters pose a challenge to the psychological continuity criterion because we can't be exactly sure what psychological states are present during their time as animals or during their "regular" lives as human beings.

For instance, when Sookie decides one evening to take home the collie who has been lurking around Merlotte's (and who, unknown both to her and to the viewers at this point in the season, is really Sam), she needs to find a name for him. When she suggests Buffy, collie-Sam growls his disapproval. After similar reactions to her other suggestions, she finally settles on Dean. That collie-Sam expressed a reaction to the names Sookie suggested seems to indicate some psychological continuity between Sam in his animal form and his human self. Sam also retains memories of what happens during the times he is in animal form. Describing his experience as a bird, he says, "I'm always scared I'm going to get fried on a power line, or fly into a window."[12] However, as Sookie herself says, "I wondered what was on Sam's mind. I wondered if he retained much human thinking while he was in his favorite form. . . . Sam/Dean's eyes followed mine, but how much comprehension was in there, I just couldn't estimate."[13]

While it *seems* that Sam retains the same psychological states as a human when he is in animal form, we cannot be sure. In *Living Dead in Dallas*, the second book of the Southern Vampire Mysteries, Sookie's investigation of a murder leads her to a wild, sexy party in Bon Temps. At a particularly tense moment, when many of the partygoers had moved out onto the porch, Andy Bellefleur comes out of the bushes, brandishing a gun. Sam wanders over in his collie form, but his only reaction is to growl at Andy. How much of Sam's humanity is present at this moment, we have to ask. If all he does is growl when a gun is pointed at his friends, how sure can we be that he retains the same mental faculties that he had as a human being? Maybe he's simply able to recall what happened in his animal state, but is not necessarily in touch with his humanity when in that state. We're left wondering whether collie-Sam's inaction when Andy seemed to be threatening his friends was due to human Sam not being fully present at that moment. If that's the case, if there was no real psychological continuity between Sam as a collie and as a human being, then the psychological continuity criterion of identity can't explain how Sam retains his personal identity when he shifts.

These same concerns apply to werewolves. One werewolf in particular has played an important role in Sookie's life—Alcide Herveaux. In *Dead as a Doornail*, the fifth book of the Southern Vampire Mysteries, Alcide recruits Sookie's telepathic skills to determine whether Patrick Furnan, who's vying with Alcide's father to lead the werewolf pack, is cheating. During the contest to choose the new leader, Sookie attempts to read the Weres' minds. She remarks, "I'd never tried to look inside the mind of a shifted person. With considerable anxiety, I concentrated on opening myself to their thoughts. As you might expect, the blend of human and dog thought patterns was quite challenging. At first scan I could only pick up the same kind of focus, but then I detected a difference."[14] Sookie seems to be saying that there are different thought patterns for wolves and human beings. Referring to Furnan, she remarks, "In his Were form, these were so primitive they hardly qualified as 'thoughts.'"[15] If this is the case and wolves think in a way entirely different from human beings—maybe because they think nonlinguistically—then it seems that a Were's psychological state when in wolf form must be very different from when he's in human form. If so, then the criterion of psychological continuity doesn't seem to explain how a Were could remain the same person despite the transformations he undergoes.[16] However, we *do* want to say that Weres have the same identity over time because they retain their sense of self when they shift back and forth and remember what's happened during and after a transformation.[17]

Many Parts to a Single Story: "My Life Sucks!"

Despite our difficulty in finding one single criterion to account for the persistence of personal identity across time—and not just for the identity of supernatural beings like vampires, werewolves, and shapeshifters but even for ordinary persons like ourselves—we still may feel that there must be something about us that persists through all of the changes we undergo, even if we can't really put a finger on what it is. The stages of our lives aren't just externally related to one another, like a bunch of blocks arranged in a row that don't have much in common besides being next to one another, but are somehow knit together to form our lives as a whole, with each stage or moment of our lives constituting only one small part of that encompassing whole. Some of those parts might seem pretty out of sync with the rest of our lives—maybe even as out of sync as a human life is with the life of a wolf, a dog, or a vampire—but something holds those moments together and gives them their unity. We have the intuition that having the same body, the same memories, and the same psychological states all contribute to that unity, but we've seen that none of them on its own can explain the persistence of our personal identities through all of the changes that our bodies, memories, and psychological states undergo.

"Think of your life as a long story," suggests the philosopher Theodore Sider, urging us to think in a way that already comes naturally to us. Indeed, what makes it possible for us to recognize the rambunctious and aggressive vampire Jessica as somehow the same person as the well-behaved and demure human Jessica is that we are able to view both Jessicas as extended episodes in a single story that we might call the life (and un-life) of Jessica so far. Jessica's story is unique in many ways, but it shares something with every other story that has ever been told—or lived—including your own: it has parts. As Sider observes, "We can distinguish the parts of the story concerning childhood from the parts concerning adulthood. Given enough details, there will be parts concerning individual days, minutes, or even instants."[18] Sider calls these "temporal parts," and he believes that what we really are is a composite of these parts, the sum of all of the stages of our existence. His theory is known as four-dimensionalism, because he holds that we are really four-dimensional objects, extended not only in three-dimensional space but across the fourth dimension of time as well. While at any given moment all that exists of you is just one minuscule temporal slice of the greater whole that is the story of your life, your full existence, the complete and unabridged *you*, is the sum of all your past, present, and future temporal parts.

And the same holds for Bill, Jessica, Sam, and Alcide, even if some of their parts are fanged, four-legged, or furry. They aren't reducible to their bodies, their memories, or their thoughts. Instead, they're a succession of all of the stages that have made up their complicated and multifaceted lives, in the course of which they've undergone some pretty drastic changes but still mysteriously managed to stay the same.

NOTES

1. Charlaine Harris, *Dead until Dark* (New York: Ace Books, 2001), p. 2.

2. Episode 101, "Strange Love."

3. Harris, *Dead until Dark*, p. 2.

4. Episode 202, "Keep This Party Going."

5. For a discussion of the belief that vampires have no souls, see Adam Barkman's chapter in this volume, "Does God Hate Fangs?"

6. Harris, *Dead until Dark*, 53.

7. John Locke, *An Essay Concerning Human Understanding*, ed. Peter H. Nidditch (Oxford: Oxford Univ. Press, 1975), book 2, chap. 26, pp. 18–22.

8. Ibid., pp. 9–14, 24–26.

9. Charlaine Harris, *Dead to the World* (New York: Ace Books, 2004), p. 21.

10. Harris, *Dead until Dark*, p. 53.

11. Ibid., p. 251.

12. Ibid., p. 252.

13. Charlaine Harris, *Living Dead in Dallas* (New York: Ace Books, 2002), p. 264.

14. Charlaine Harris, *Dead as a Doornail* (New York: Ace Books, 2005), p. 267.

15. Ibid., p. 205.

16. It may be pointed out that there are other elements to psychological continuity aside from just thought. For instance, we consider emotions and desires to be aspects of our psychological states. If this is the case, however, we are still left in a quandary because we cannot be sure that the emotions and desires of a Were are constant in their transformative state. Does desire operate differently in human beings from the way it does in other animals? Human beings are capable of reflecting on and constraining their desires. Are Weres? Do Weres experience emotion in the same way that human beings do? These are all problems for the psychological continuity criterion.

17. This reference to retained memories is an appeal to the memory criterion mentioned previously. As we saw, memories alone cannot constitute an individual's continued personal identity; however, memory does seem to play some sort of role in a person's sense of self.

18. Theodore Sider, *Four-Dimensionalism: An Ontology of Persistence and Time* (Oxford: Oxford Univ. Press, 2001), p. 1.

CONTRIBUTORS

"I Don't Know Who You Think You Are, but Before the Night Is Through . . ."

Robert Arp works as a contractor for the U.S. Air Force building ontologies (in the information science sense) and has interests in philosophy of biology and philosophy and pop culture as well. His latest books include *Philosophy of Biology: An Anthology* (2009), *Contemporary Debates in Philosophy of Biology* (2009), and *Batman and Philosophy* (2008), all published by Wiley. He was once bitten by a so-called child of the night—a sinister, sneaky, blood-sucking . . . mosquito.

Adam Barkman is assistant professor of philosophy at Redeemer University College. He is the author of *C. S. Lewis and Philosophy as a Way of Life* (Zossima Press, 2009) and *Through Common Things* (Winged Lion, 2010) and is the coeditor of *Manga and Philosophy* (Open Court, 2010). He has also written nine chapters for books in the Philosophy and Pop Culture series. Although crosses apparently don't keep vampires at bay the way they used to, Adam, being a dedicated Christian, still keeps one hanging on the wall as a reminder of the Light . . . and just in case.

Ariadne Blayde is currently pursuing her BA at Fordham University in New York City. A published playwright who hopes to write for television someday, she is thrilled to have the opportunity to contribute to this volume. She has many years of experience with vampires and philosophy, as her coauthor (and father) George Dunn introduced her at an early age to *Buffy the Vampire Slayer*, apparently as an excuse to fill her ears with a running harangue on the ethics and metaphysics of vampire slayage.

Patricia Brace is a professor of art history at Southwest Minnesota State University, in Marshall, Minnesota. With Robert Arp, she contributed a chapter to the Blackwell volume *Lost and Philosophy: The Island Has Its Reasons* (2008) and a chapter on logic in the films of David Lynch in the proposed University Press of Kentucky project *The Philosophy of David Lynch*. Pat would like to meet Nordic vampire Eric Northman so she could discuss Viking interlace motifs on drakkar ship prows with him . . . and other things.

Kevin J. Corn teaches in the Department of Philosophy and Religion at the University of Indianapolis. Once a simple historian of religious movements, he has published works focused on themes of middle-class respectability and moral reform. Since that time, he has fallen in among philosophers, married into a family of Transylvanians, and taken a basement office where he writes obsessively about blood sacrifice, sacred pain, and holy war.

Lillian E. Craton is assistant professor of English literature at Lander University in Greenwood, South Carolina. Her true love is Victorian literature, and her forthcoming book is titled *The Victorian Freak Show: Physical Difference in Nineteenth-Century Fiction* (Cambia Press, 2009). Like Sookie, she lives in a quirky old house on a lonely tract of farmland deep in the rural South, although her neighbors all claim to be human.

Jennifer Culver is an associate professor at the University of Texas at Dallas and contributed to *Terminator and Philosophy* (Wiley, 2009). Jennifer also teaches high school, a place where one never knows exactly what may be found in the hallways!

Fred Curry earned his PhD from Bowling Green State University in the spring of 2007. Since then he has continued teaching philosophy at BGSU both as an adjunct and as a full-time instructor. His primary areas of specialization include philosophy of biology and philosophy of mind. He also has a strong interest in the convergence of philosophy, neurology, and computer science, in terms of the creation of both artificial intelligence and artificial life. He hopes to one day prove strong AI theorists correct by building the first true artificially conscious machine out of pots and pans in his basement. He is currently working on the first step in this plan by trying to rent a property with a basement (where he promises not keep vampires prisoner . . . poor Eddie).

William M. Curtis is an assistant professor of political science at the University of Portland. His research interests include contemporary liberal theory, modern political philosophy, and constitutional law and theory. He is currently working on a manuscript about philosopher Richard Rorty's political philosophy and its relationship to literary criticism. He would definitely venture into Fangtasia if given the chance, and thinks that Eric Northman is easily the funniest character in *True Blood*.

George A. Dunn teaches philosophy at the University of Indianapolis, Indiana–Purdue University in Indianapolis, and the Ningbo Institute of Technology in the People's Republic of China. An editor of this volume and frequent contributor to the Wiley Pop Culture and Philosophy Series, he wants it on record that he does *not* endorse the philosophy of Amy Burley. In particular, he does not believe that playing our part in the "circle of life" means we can wantonly kill other sentient beings, nor does he believe that *thanking* a captive vampire as you drink his blood makes it right.

Joseph J. Foy is an assistant professor of political science at the University of Wisconsin–Waukesha. Foy is the editor of the John G. Cawelti Award–winning book *Homer Simpson Goes to Washington: American Politics through Popular Culture* (University of Kentucky Press, 2008) and coeditor of the follow-up *Homer Simpson Marches on Washington: Dissent through American Popular Culture* (University of Kentucky Press, 2010). In his spare time, Joe applies his political knowledge to lobbying and can't understand why members of Congress always hang up when he raises questions about equal rights for the undead.

Sarah Grubb is a philosophy instructor at Waubonsee Community College in Illinois. She holds a BA in philosophy from Rutgers University and an MA in philosophy from Northern Illinois University. While she has a bartending license, Sarah would be very hesitant about ever applying for a job at Merlotte's, having heard Bon Temps has an unusually high mortality rate.

Ron Hirschbein has a fascination with Freud that began with Ron's first book, *Newest Weapons/Oldest Psychology* (Peter Lang, 1989), an account of the irrational forces driving the nuclear arms race. While a visiting professor at University of California campuses in San Diego and Berkeley and at the United Nations University in Austria, he pursued his controversial account of international crises in *What If They Gave a Crisis and Nobody Came?* (Praeger, 1997). He created programs in war and peace studies at his home campus, California State University–Chico, where he's semiretired. He currently mentors PhD candidates at Walden University's School of Public Administration and has served two terms as president of Concerned Philosophers for Peace, the largest philosophic organization concerned with the causes of war and prospects for peace. None of his blood relatives are vampires.

Rebecca Housel has edited three books in the Wiley Philosophy and Pop Culture Series, including *Twilight and Philosophy* (2009) and *X-Men and Philosophy* (2009), both with J. Jeremy Wisnewski, and was a professor of popular culture, film, and writing for fifteen years before shapeshifting into a full-time writer/editor. Rebecca has also written articles on the philosophy of super-heroes, Iron Man, poker, and Monty Python. Her abilities as a "supe" have (fortunately) kept her from being eaten by vampires for some time now, though not for lack of trying by the vamps. Damn fairy blood . . .

Kathryn E. Jonell is a graduate of Kennesaw State University and a freelance editor, and is currently trying to find opportunities to be a spy or a graduate student or both at the same time. She has long been involved in Internet fandom for many books and television shows. Her grandfather was from Transylvania, she inexplicably always has deathly cold fingers, and she bursts into flames in direct sunlight; tests as to whether she is a vampire have been thus far inconclusive.

Bruce A. McClelland is a poet, scholar, and translator who lives in Virginia and has been thinking and writing seriously about vampires for over thirty years. He has a doctorate in Slavic folklore from the University of Virginia, having written a dissertation titled *Sacrifice, Scapegoat, Vampire: The Social and Religious Origins of the Bulgarian Folkloric Vampire*. His most recent book is *Slayers and Their Vampires: A Cultural History of Killing the Dead* (University of Michigan, 2006). For obvious reasons, he uses Jace Everett's "Bad Things" as the ringtone for his wife.

Susan Peppers-Bates is associate professor of philosophy at Stetson University in Florida. She recently published *Nicolas Malebranche: Freedom in an Occasionalist World* (Continuum Press, 2009). A sci-fi/fantasy geek from early adolescence, she is relieved to come out of the closet with her fondness for vampires— although she had to promise her worried department chair that she would not write her next book on the metaphysics of the undead—maybe after she's a full professor. When not at work, she plays with her five-year-old daughter, Anne-Marie, prepares for the birth of her second daughter, Sophia Frances, and chews on philosophical puzzles with her husband, Todd (occasionally nibbling his neck).

Christopher Robichaud is an instructor in public policy at the Harvard Kennedy School of Government. For his preschool Career Day, he insisted on dressing as Count Dracula. So began his love affair with vampires. Years later, that romance blossomed when he acted in an independent vampire movie. He was delighted that the love affair continued with an opportunity to contribute to this volume. In the undead world of *True Blood*, Chris may not want to *do* bad things with you, but he certainly wants to *think* about what, if anything, makes them bad in the first place.

Joshua Rust is an assistant professor of philosophy at Stetson University. He is the author of two books on John Searle published by Continuum Press, as well as a coauthor of articles that inquire into whether ethicists are, in fact, more ethical than other philosophers. Because he likes sinking his teeth into so many philosophical topics, he can't help but feel some regret about the limits mere mortality place on him. Why aren't more vampires philosophers?

Andrew Terjesen is an assistant professor of philosophy at Rhodes College—the alma mater of Charlaine Harris. He had previously taught at Washington and Lee University and Austin College. He has contributed to several volumes of Wiley's Philosophy and Pop Culture Series, including *Twilight and Philosophy* (2009) and *Iron Man and Philosophy* (2010), as well as to their Philosophy for Everyone Series with an essay in the forthcoming *Serial Killers and Philosophy*. However, having lived and worked at "ground zero" for the creation of the Southern Vampire Mysteries, he feels all of this has been but a prelude to writing his chapter in this book. In his "real" job, he spends a lot of time thinking about business ethics. Writing about Eric Northman was a nice respite from those bloodsuckers.

Jenny Terjesen lives in Memphis, Tennessee. When she's not having long Sookie Stackhouse discussions with her sister Rachel Whisnant (whose total obsession with the Southern Vampire Mysteries compelled Jenny to read them all) or composing an essay for *Twilight and Philosophy* (Wiley, 2009), she works in human resources. Jenny wonders if vampirism would qualify for protection from employment discrimination as a disability under the newest provisions of the Americans with Disabilities Act. She thinks it might.

INDEX

Sookie's Words of the Day